From the Author of *Children of the Core*

KRIS L. NIELSEN

UNCOMMON

*The Grassroots Movement to
Save our Children and Their Schools*

Foreword by Peggy Robertson

UNCOMMON

UNCOMMON

Copyright © 2013 Kris L. Nielsen

For more information: http://www.childrenofthecore.com
Contact the author by email: klnielsen74@gmail.com.

ISBN-10: 1489556044
ISBN-13: 978-1489556042

Cover art created by Danielle Boudet

Printed in the United States of America

Praise for *Children of the Core*

"Nielsen does an excellent job of clearly demonstrating how conservative, profit-minded coalitions are taking over curricular and assessment elements of public education. Children of the Core *is accessible to wide audience, making it suitable for both academics and for parents who have concerns about the amount of testing that has infiltrated their children's schools. This book is helpful for anyone who wants to understand how the coalition of corporations and politicians are moving to privatizing education.*"

Gary Weilbacher

"This book has laid out an extensive case for opposing current practices in education which blame teachers, students and schools for "poor performance" and it offers a multitude of resources for both educators and parents to access to further explore his reasoning and possible solutions. This book is a 'wake up' call to all who are interested in opposing the corporate takeover of public education in America. A must read!"

Martha H. Myers

"I found this book to be an honest account, backed up by ample research, of what Common Core State Standards are and how dangerous they are to the educational system in the U.S. Easy to read and very informative. A must read for anyone wanting information to share with their neighbors."

Dr. Darwin Lawson

CONTENTS

FOREWORD

It is hard to believe that a year has gone by since I first posted Kris's teaching resignation letter on our website at United Opt Out National. I met Kris on Facebook in August of 2012, and his decision to resign from his teaching position in October immediately led him down the activist path. He has taken on Common Core in his brilliant book, *Children of the Core*, and now he tackles the bigger picture of corporate education reform, while keeping the heart of this fight front and center: this is an attack on *our children*.

As parents, activists, and educators who are awake to this attack, this is the one constant upon which we all agree. Kris takes this constant and brings to the forefront the key players who have launched this corporate takeover while also sharing activist stories from the brave leadership of many who are fighting back. Activism can take many forms. Each of us moves forward using our strengths to wake the public and help them see how they are being robbed of what is rightfully theirs—a fully-funded, equitable public education for all children.

Kris's activism takes its form in writing, which is clear, engaging, and to the point. And if you ever get to meet him in person, he is an amazing speaker. He will keep you laughing at the most crucial times when you feel the need to blink back tears.

These are our children and they should not be suffering under these corporate, politically-endorsed mandates. We have a hard road ahead of us. Kris speaks the truth and does so in a manner that is accessible to all. He shares models that we can emulate in our communities, while also filling our toolkit with the knowledge of the bigger picture. Read Kris's book and share it with your neighbors. Spread the wealth of knowledge. Now is the time for mass action. As a founder of United Opt Out National, I believe that resistance can and will succeed as parents, teachers, students and citizens stand up together. Let the revolution begin!

Peggy Robertson
www.pegwithpen.com
www.unitedoptout.com

A NOTE FROM A TEACHER

You want to know what's wrong with education in the U.S.? This. Exactly this.

Politicians and CEOs are not educational experts. Teachers are. We do not need biosensors to tell us when children are engaged in a lesson. We learned how to do that in college. Through the magical powers of observation.

So not only do these non-experts distrust our ability to create our own curriculum, they now also distrust our ability to interpret what is going on in our classrooms and adjust our plans accordingly.

Would you trust a CEO or a politician to perform your surgeries? Your dental work? How about your car maintenance? Solve murder cases? Color your hair? Of course not. You want the expert, and you'd like her to not have ten extra non-expert hands in the way.

I am the professional you want teaching your kid. I've proven my expertise by successfully completing four years of content and pedagogy study, two internships, at least five written *PRAXIS* tests, a year of mentoring and observations (by school, university, and state personnel), a portfolio containing evidence of my teaching ability, three probationary years, and my continued acquisition of far over the required 60 hours of professional development every summer. And because I strive for true excellence, I have also earned a Master's degree and additional certifications, including one which taught me the unique needs of teaching English Language Learners.

Do you want me able to put to use all of the pedagogical knowledge I gained when I earned my degrees? Because right now, I can't. My time has been taken up by all of these distractions from non-educators. And time is the true resource we are lacking. Time and the autonomy required to put our expertise to use.

If you want education to improve, you have to give it back to the experts.

Elizabeth Rollans

ACKNOWLEDGEMENTS

Since the release of *Children of the Core*, I found myself working more closely with old friends and meeting scores of new friends, who I was proud to stand alongside in this ongoing grassroots movement to save our children and their schools. There is power in numbers and, thankfully, those numbers have been with me the whole way through this project—my second—directing me to resources, people, and stories that are truly helpful and even inspiring. This book seemed to go a little quicker than the last one, even though it's longer and much more in-depth and involved. That's because my "team" grew larger and the brains behind this movement are starting to truly grasp what's happening around here.

I felt a little bad asking Peggy Robertson to take the time to write the foreword for this book, since she's the busiest person in the entire world. She's a wealth of knowledge and support, and if you haven't yet visited the United Opt Out website, you're missing out. It may be the most important, time-saving resource you use this year.

In April, I went to speak and listen at the Occupy DOE 2.0 protest rally in Washington, D.C., and I met face-to-face with several people who have my gratitude. Thanks to Diane Ravitch for her continued support of all of us, and her fearless role modeling for speaking truth to power. Shaun Johnson and Tim Slekar continue to sit in my corner, and I'm proud to be a part of their blogging team. I thank Morna McDermott for her hard work digging up information and presenting so cogently, so that I and many others can make the connections that are affecting us so greatly and for spreading the truth through video. Awesome stuff! Thanks to Elizabeth Lynch, who is not only a true fighter and defender of kids, but also a person whom I admire and learn from every encounter—virtually or personally. Michelle Gunderson, you are the definition of grassroots fighter.

The two most important people, I believe, in getting me really fired up and prepared to finish this project were the cofounders of Parents and Teachers Against Common Core (P-TACC). Jeanine Baxter-Cozzetti and Sara Wottawa are the most feared team in Long Island education reform circles. Sara can't know enough how much we all appreciate her tireless research, and how invaluable the information is to my work as I write and speak to others.

Thanks to Dr. Mark Naison for the passionate speeches, the useful advice, and the support. And we all should raise our glasses to his advocacy for public education and the children whom we serve. Dr. Naison is a revolutionary, and I'm proud to call him my friend.

If this struggle were a Hollywood-style war movie, Gail Richmond and I would be hobbling out of the smoke, bruised and battered, propping each other up. Damaged and victorious. Thank you, Gail, for everything. You are a true optimist and one of my biggest heroes!

Thanks to the two superheroes of New York State test refusal, Eric Mihelbergel and Chris Cerrone. New York State needs you, and you come through for us every time. You are true rockstars, and I look up to both of you.

Thank you to the parent-warriors who have given me personal accounts and information to follow as the fight goes on. Danielle Boudet is one of the most dedicated parents and wonderful writers I've known, and Jeanette Deutermann possesses more power and charisma than I could ever muster, which led the parent refusal movement to new heights in Long Island. You both are inspirational!

Thanks to the parents of Douglas County, Colorado, who are in the struggle for the fate of their community, for elevating me and showing me a whole face to the ugliness. Stefanie Fuhr and everyone at Voices for Public Education, thanks!

And here is the big list of those who come to mind when I think of who is responsible for getting me through this latest project: Donna Mace, Stephen Krashen, Candaloo Gonzalez, Rosemarie Jensen, Mike Rockow, Nikhil Goyal, Susan DuFresne (master of the meme), Joan Kramer, Alicia Palifka (and her future-president son), Susan Jennifer, Deborah Lang, Deborah Carter, Deb Howard (thanks for the letter), Anthony Cody, Michelle Doorey, and Meg Norris.

To the brave Heather Ryder, the innovative Katie Lapham, the intelligent Michael Bohr. Thanks to Sara Attleson, Yvonne Gasperino, Kathleen Knauth, Peter Dewitt, Jennifer Fatone, Autumn Cook, Keri Lynn, Ralph Ratto, Kuhio Kane, Brian Fay, Mary Bieger, Leonie Haimson, Christel Swasey, Steve Shrey, Dora Taylor, Jennifer Gallegos, Iain Coggins, Christine McCartney, Lisa Muntean, Claudia Swisher, Ceresta Smith, Nora McNamara, Alisa Ellis, Angela Weinzinger, Denisha Jones, Lori Atkinson—every one of you are responsible for getting me to think a little deeper, look a little closer, and follow some new trail to the end. Thank you all.

I could go on and on, but I'm sure you all want to get right to it. Know that every parent and teacher and student with whom I've had contact has influenced me in some way that helps to continue my passion for this fight. You are so important, and someday, we will have our reward.

Oh, and thank you the principal who just hired me and got me back into the game. I can't wait to get started! I'm happy you've either never heard of me or look forward to having my fight in your district.

PREFACE

In February of 2013, Monica, a New York parent of two boys, started to notice some troubling behaviors in her seven-year-old son, Ryan. Actually, the behaviors seemed familiar to her, and she remembered the odd feeling she was feeling in her stomach from about the same time the previous year. This is a gut-feeling that many parents start to feel when they know something just isn't right with their kids. She could sense that something was amiss with her son and he either didn't want to or didn't know how to express it to her. Sometimes he would start tearing up during homework time or while reading. Sometimes he would start to get angry while doing very simple tasks, like loading the dishwasher.

Monica would ask Ryan every day how things were going. After the expected shrug and "fine," she would ask more specific questions about friends, school, home, her cooking, his physical well-being, even (at the age of seven), girls. Friends, home, and her cooking all got responses that caused Monica no worry. When she asked passive questions about girls, he would grimace and stick out his tongue. (Whew!) When she would ask about school, he would shrug.

"You do bring home a lot of homework. Is it the work? Is it too hard?"

Shrug.

"Is anybody giving you a hard time? Do you feel safe?"

Shrug. Nod.

Monica's concern, in this day of seemingly increased incidence of bullying, was that her son was perhaps victimized by peers. We know that many cases of bullying tend to go unreported for long periods of time, until a teacher or parent notices new symptoms or the acts themselves, and some incidents may go unnoticed until the unthinkable happens. So, Monica kept pressing. After enough time and questioning, she concluded that her child was not a victim of peer bullying.

The day she found out what was really wrong was the day that she became a parent activist.

"I'm tired of feeling stupid!"

The outburst had caught Monica by surprise. Her son was in tears and started sobbing again after yelling those terrible words. She hugged her son tight and told him everything was okay. She listened as her son opened the floodgates of feelings, fears, frustrations, and anger. Ryan has dyslexia, which he tends to manage quite well when he's allowed to use strategies that work for him and work at his own pace. Unfortunately, his classroom had been transformed that year, due to the statewide implementation of Common Core and the new high-stakes testing that New York State Education Department had ordered to be aligned to those standards.

This put new pressures on every level of the system, most of all, the students. Monica knows her son is incredibly bright, curious, creative, and optimistic. He loves science and he loves to read, even though it proves challenging at times. He is masterful with comprehension and is a very good writer for his age. With the changes prescribed from the top, the classroom is no longer a safe and welcoming place for kids like Ryan. There is serious pressure for teachers to get all of their students to the same place, using the same techniques, with the same materials, and at the same time. Ryan, being a child who needs extra time to read, is at risk of being left behind. But, even worse than that, Ryan is a child who is at risk of being tired of knowing that he is not cutting it, that he is not performing the way that the current education reformers in America expect him to, which will someday lead to his quitting.

Ryan is one of at least a dozen early elementary kids that I have personally heard tearfully say that they don't want to go to school anymore. It's confusing, it's difficult, it's boring, it's stressful, no one seems happy, there's not really anything interesting happening. "I'm tired of feeling stupid."

Teachers see it happening. They speak up about it, and they risk sanctions. I know of two elementary teachers who have questioned the system a little too passionately and have been suspended. I know of several teachers who have been warned by superiors or union leaders to tone down their statements and their questions, lest they be targeted for disciplinary actions.

The changes that have been leading up to these depressing events have placed the burden upon the shoulders of children. Parents, last year and this year, started to take notice. And they started to take action.

In April and May of 2013, something extraordinary happened, the likes of which had never been seen before. New York State, which was among the first states to align their state standardized tests to the new Common Core State Standards, saw the largest boycott of such tests in American history. It was clear early on that New York had no legislative procedure for "opting out" of the tests (the movement was originally known as New York Opt Out), so thousands of parents and students chose to *refuse* to participate in the statewide testing, making use of a procedural "loophole" in the grading structure of the test. That loophole said that if a student refused to take the test, for whatever reason, the test would be marked as a refusal and there would be no meaningful score[1]. The test and answer sheet would be discarded without moving to the next phase of scoring and data collection.

Thanks to the tireless advocacy and research of a small band of parent coordinators, the fledgling statewide movement grew into the thousands in a matter of weeks. From Buffalo in the west to Long Island communities in the east, over ten thousand students refused to take the English or math tests over that two-week period. Hundreds more kept up the momentum and refused to participate in benchmark exams, field tests, and other state- and district-mandated tests for the remainder of the year. The parent and student activists were praised as well as chastised by school officials, and they got the attention of the media and the rest of the country. Soon after, parents and students in several other states began to organize and grow opt out groups to try to make the same splash in their own communities. Some saw success, others saw little of anything, and still others were met with stiff resistance from their state education departments.

The one question that the media kept asking parents and students was: why? What was the reasoning behind this boycott? Before we get to the *real* answers, given by *real* parents, let's spend some time on the spin that was offered by the New York State Education Department (NYSED), and other New York education officials, in response to the grassroots parent movement. You'll find right away that there was an obvious and coordinated effort to slander, discredit, and insult these brave and caring parents. I'm sure that many of these statements were also heard around the rest of the country, as parents attempted to stand up for their kids.

NYSED: Parents don't care about their kids' progress

Dennis Tompkins, a spokesman for the New York State Education Department, made some parents' blood start to boil when he said, "Parents who keep their children from these tests are essentially saying 'I don't want to know where my child stands, in objective terms, on the path to college and career readiness' and we think that's doing them a real disservice."[2]

What Dennis is effectively saying here is that teachers are worthless in regards to teaching *and* assessing your kids. He believes that parents are actually hurting their own kids by allowing teachers–who spend hours and days with their students, watching and listening and evaluating–to assess kids. Here's a history tidbit: teachers have been objectively (meaning, *quantitatively*) and *qualitatively* measuring students' progress for a very long time. And if there's one thing we've already found out over the past decade, it's that standardized tests do not objectively measure student progress. When parents want to know how their kids are doing in school, there has been one place they have gone to consistently get that information: from the educators who are educating them inside the walls of the school, not from a statewide database that contains scale scores and item analyses based on test scores.

Even worse, he's saying that opt-out parents are doing a bad job of parenting and what they *should* be doing is listening to the state for the best methods in education. The idea that state officials would insult the motives of parents is baffling. These are not reactionaries; these are intelligent parents who did their research, expressed their concerns numerous times to those state officials, and decided to take matters into their own hands after receiving no response. Again, the state education officials running the testing scheme had many, many opportunities to respond meaningfully or engage in dialogue about parent concerns. They chose to ignore those parents. When parents know something isn't working--and, in fact, is harmful to the well-being of their children--and the people responsible refuse to discuss it, those parents are going to seek another way to stop it. And they did.

New York City Department of Education: We should expect that our kids feel pain

Dennis Walcott, New York City Chancellor of Schools, famously stated that he knows the tests will be incredibly difficult and that several students will not pass, which may hurt their little hearts and minds, but "it's time to rip the Band-Aid off, and we have a responsibility to rip that Band-Aid off."[3]

The first question: *What Band-Aid?* Does this imply that our schools and our kids are figuratively bleeding and there is some temporary tourniquet keeping our education system from bleeding out and falling apart? If so, then the analogy is sort of clever, in a not-so-innovative way. First of all, the bleeding--the crisis--has not been defined outside of test scores, and those have actually been *increasing* nationwide, as well as in New York State. Assuming that there was some actual education crisis and that the only way to solve the problem was to create harder tests, then ripping the Band-Aid off with tests that we know our kids are going to fail is still not a cure. This assumes that the Common Core State Standards and the accompanying test regiments are like Neosporin, which can speed the healing. Wrong. You can't heal a wound by causing more damage. Especially since there aren't any gaping wounds regarding education, other than those that have been inflicted by the education chiefs to begin with.

Whatever the crisis is supposed to be—manufactured or not—reactionary policies, like increased testing, won't work. What started to work was when we allowed educators and administrators and parents to start engaging in the conversation, which was happening in the 1990s and mid-2000s, believe it or not, even during the NCLB years. Something about that system made "reformers" very uncomfortable, so they told us that we were all failing (we weren't), that our kids were dumber than the rest of the kids in the world (they aren't), and that teachers are the cause (they are most certainly not). If there was a wound prior to 2008, it was healing on its own through careful research and tender loving care. The wound that Walcott refers to, from which the Band-Aid needs to be quickly removed, is self-inflicted by the educational bureaucracy--and is pretty much imaginary, as well.

I believe that by suggesting we "rip off the Band-Aid," what Walcott is really suggesting is roughly the same as the idea Merryl Tisch (see below) had of pushing kids into the deep-end of the pool. I get what they're trying to convey, but their metaphors just seem to get creepier and creepier.

NYSED: Parents are a bad influence on their children

Ken Wagner, Associate Commissioner of NYSED, told the *New York Times* that he was worried that the concerns of parents were rubbing off on their children, causing kids to suffer anxiety about the state tests. He's then quoted as saying, "My heart goes out to any kid that's [sic] suffering stress or anxiety, but *we have to think very strategically about the messages that students are getting from the adults they are around"* (emphasis added).[4]

Two major problems with this: (1) the parent reaction was a direct result of kids' anxieties and fears, not the other way around; and (2) who gets to make the "strategy" regarding what messages kids get to hear from their concerned parents? If there's one thing that's getting very tiring around here, it's listening to state and Federal officials trying to tell parents how to parent. It's especially tiring because the parental "advice" they're offering has nothing to do with kids—it has only to do with not making their corporate buddies mad. To suggest that parents use strategy in keeping their kids in line with bad education policy is, in itself, negligent.

Look again at that italicized part of Mr. Wagner's statement. This has been a trend in politics for a little while, although it's difficult to determine when it really started. To residents of New York, it's obvious that it has become a "nanny state," where government leaders have determined that people can't take care of themselves, so they need to increasingly find ways to pass laws to micromanage human behavior. It's been getting worse and has been begun to take hold pretty much everywhere. Government thinks it knows better how to be a parent than the parents of America. It's in the president's speeches, it's in the laws of several states, and it's in the quick-and-quiet way that education policies and initiatives are snuck into schools under parents' radars while they aren't looking. The "strategy" that Mr. Wagner is referring to is the one that government has decided to create to make sure that parents are guided by the hand as they raise their kids, or to bypass the parents altogether. It seems that in Mr. Wagner's ideal state, the government would strategically determine what kids are allowed to hear from their parents.

One has to wonder what his strategy regarding consequences would be for those parents who express concerns of the state's policies in front of their kids. After all, some districts had decided that opt-out parents were worthy of disciplinary actions, such as reporting them to child protective services and having their children banned from outside school-sponsored activities as punishment.

Multiple: Without the state tests, children will never be ready for college and/or careers

Let's use Ken Wagner again, from the same *New York Times* article as above. (However, this line has been repeated *ad nauseum* by many different officials.) We hear it over and over again. The Common Core State Standards are the "answer" to our kids' success in college and the workforce (that one was from State Education Commissioner, John King[5]). The most primary issue with this cheap and overused line is that there is no evidence, whatsoever, to back it up. The standards have never been tested, never been shown effective in reaching the goals that are propagandized, and have actually been deemed inappropriate for the 21st century, if you use models and statements from other countries as examples.

And the tests are not designed for *kids*. They do not evaluate *kids*. They aren't designed to track individual academic student progress (again, a statement from John King). Bill Gates, on the other hand, *does* want to use them to track our kids, but not in the way that we would like. That'll be discussed in chapter 2.

This "college and career" statement also makes a blanket assumption about all kids. In order for our students to get into college, they must learn everything in the standards and pass tests based on those standards. You know who increasingly doesn't care about state (or national) standardized tests? Ask your closest university.

New York Board of Regents: Stressing your kids to the point of vomiting is healthy.

Merryl Tisch, who is also not technically part of NYSED, is the Chancellor of the Board of New York Regents. She was seen in a recent *Wall Street Journal* piece responding to reports from principals, teachers, students, and parents of kids breaking down crying during and after tests, vomiting during tests, and not wanting the leave the bathroom—all due to the anxieties and stress of the overwhelming English-Language Arts testing during the previous three days. Her response was that she had visited several schools and only saw one kid crying. The *Wall Street Journal* then goes on:

> But she called it a "healthy problem." It would be worse, she said, if tests were described as unfair or poorly done. Last year, for example, the state had to toss out questions

related to a passage that was widely ridiculed for being confusing. "I would be so bold as to say they were better than most people expected them to be," she said.[6]

So, it's healthy for our kids to suffer this way, according to the obviously out-of-touch and stone-hearted Tisch. The evidence was piling up during the testing period that those exams were unfair and poorly done, and several questions had invalid distractors or were recycled from previous years. I joined the growing camp of people with test design experience who suggested that this year's tests were not just poorly done and unfair (which we can only assume from the stories we've heard, since we can't see the tests for at least another year), they were a flat-out disaster. They were, as blogger Chris Cerrone has written, a #fail–with a hashtag!

NYSED: Even though the tests don't mean anything for students, they should do them anyway. Because they're hard.

John King, Commissioner of New York State Education Department told parents that they should make their kids take the tests due to their "character-building" design. You can find many stories of Dr. King repeating the same things as his cohorts above. But what really gets our goat is his nerve when trying to tell New York parents how to educate their kids, and then doing the complete opposite.

He tells us, as parents, that we should encourage our kids to try things that are hard, while letting them know that the most important thing is that they tried their best.[7]

Hey parents: is there anyone out there who doesn't do this on a pretty consistent basis?

But here's the thing: we don't ever tell them, for months on end, that if they don't do well on something, then their teachers will get a bad grade and that their schools will suffer and they may even have to give up some fun classes and activities because, if you can't pass the tests like a normal kid, you're going to have to take extra math and reading classes. These are kids. They aren't competitive employees or other corporate property.

We know, thanks the *New York Times*, that John King's own children don't take the same state tests as public school kids do. They don't go to a school that's drowning in the Common Core.[8] That's very, very confusing to New York citizens. If the Common Core is the "answer" to college and career readiness, and the state tests are the only objective way to determine if kids are going to make it, then are John King's kids doomed?

As far back as I can conjure, my family lineage is a product of public education. My own education spans six states, which tends to personally and anecdotally discredit the argument for the need of common standards nationwide to keep kids from losing ground. I am an anecdotal argument that common national standards aren't necessary to succeed in college and career. My extended family did and are doing pretty well. I grew up among scholars, scientists, auto mechanics, service workers, computer scientists, waitresses, teachers, church workers, engineers, and other assorted vocations—just in my own family. I finished high school a semester late, due to my own shortcomings, and worked in three very distinct fields before I finally settled on my niche: teaching. In other words, I didn't know what I really wanted to be when I grew until I was about 28 years old. And I see nothing wrong with that. That should be a badge of honor for the public school system that educated me. I was given the skills, knowledge, and flexibility to work just about anywhere, with a little extra training.

Most importantly, my ancestors and I were free to make the choices we made by ourselves. We didn't have to rely on test scores or other data to keep us on track to some predestined goal. We certainly didn't have to wait for the government to tell us how to proceed with our lives.

However, my daughters didn't see the same thing. Most of the time they spent in school was under the reworked Elementary and Secondary Education Act (No Child Left Behind). All three of them dropped out for various reasons and are now pursuing college programs with interest and vitality. My youngest daughter, who is going to start college at the age of 16, found that her hard work and creativity towards solving problems was not moving her to where she felt she needed to go. As a teacher and a parent, I agreed. She left two years of AP classes and top 5% test scores behind, took a GED, and never looked back. She wants to be a neuroscientist, and at the rate she's going, she'll have a Ph.D. before she's 25.

I also have a two-year-old ball of energy moving rapidly closer to entering the school system. If Race to the Top is allowed to continue on its present course, my adaptive, curious, intelligent young son will take his first standardized test in two years--at the preschool level. I believe he would have to start getting prepared for that even earlier.

So, why did so many other parents across the country decide to let their children refuse to take the state standardized tests? Why was there a movement in the first place? Let's consider the truths as they were spelled out by parents and students. The following are real statements from real parents. I have only edited for grammar, punctuation, or clarity.

Parent: This is bad for our kids and it's not fair to teachers

My battle started with my 5th grader when I knew that there was something wrong (auditory processing or dyslexia), and we just hadn't figured it out yet. As testing time grew near, and his anxiety level skyrocketed, I found out about [the New York Opt Out group] and everything that was going on. I opted him out because I do not believe in the high-stakes testing and the stress and anxiety it is causing our children. I also do not believe in teaching to a test. In the meantime, we have found out that he does in fact have auditory processing [challenges] and a very high likelihood of also having dyslexia. He will end up with a 504 plan, with help on testing, mostly because of difficulty understanding questions. Even his teachers say that he understands the concepts and materials but does not understand questions on tests without help and clarification. He is a perfect example of a child who has learned all year, but whose teachers would be negatively affected by high-stakes testing, and it is not fair.

Parent: The testing mania has broken the system, and we want to help fix it

My 4th and 7th grade daughters refused, along with my 2nd grade son refusing the [Student Learning Objectives tests]. I'm opposed to the tests for all the popular and obvious reasons (unreliable data, lost instruction time, biased toward minorities, narrowing curriculum, etc.), but mostly we refused because I didn't want to perpetuate the problem, but rather be part of the solution. I realize that bringing about lasting social change means that things will get worse before they get better. We owe it to the kids that are currently living this nightmare called public education to do something immediate.

Parents: The Common Core and the tests have ruined school for some kids

I have a different spin on this in a lot of ways, as I didn't refuse the tests. But instead, I pulled my son out of school and started homeschooling. I felt refusing tests wasn't going to do the job for us. He would have still been subjected to all the pre-testing, [test preparations], and the Common Core [Standards]. It was getting out of hand and I wasn't willing to keep him suffocated by this nonsense until we are "heard."

* * *

We actually withdrew our son from public schools this year. He did take the tests in 3rd grade and did ok. However, many factors made us give him the option to homeschool as he was unhappy and wanted out. It became clear to us that no child should call himself an "idiot" or "stupid," and that is how he was feeling. It was the best decision we ever made and he is fortunate we can do this for him. Most kids have to stay in school and suffer.

Since the February release of *Children of the Core*, the growth of the movement to remove and block destructive education "reform" policies has been impressive in both strength and in numbers. Voices began filling the airwaves, blogosphere, and social media sites where before there was relative silence. Parents began talking, teachers began questioning, and pundits began speculating. Not everything has been on topic or on the level, but the fact that the conversation has been spreading and that the anger is now apparent speaks to the fact that we know something's not right and those who are in control are not being very forthcoming.

I have an idea: let's get states to start pulling out of Race to the Top (which is costing them more money than they're getting), get rid of the mandates that came with it, hold governors' feet to the fire to start funding our kids' schools fairly and fully, and get back to the business of teaching our children for the future. Not the Bill Gates version of the future; the *real* version.

The opt-out movement was only the beginning, and it was an important beginning. Opting out sent the message to state education officials that parents were waking up to the fact that something isn't right with the way education is working for our kids or their teachers. Even more important, it stills serves as the boycott—the ongoing statement that we are determined to starve the corporations of what they hunger after the most: our kids' data. And hungry they are. Since May, parents and teachers have reported surveys and other collection tools asking for a myriad of different types of information, from access to personal health records to incriminating questionnaires regarding drug use to long forms asking for income- and home-related issues. The message of advice that we continue to give parents and students is always the same: *deny them the data.*

But this goes so much deeper than making our kids suffer through test preparation and the tests themselves. Deeper, even, than the standardization of learning in preparation for those tests. There is a very large movement at work at the Federal and state levels, which have locked local districts and schools into a game they can't possibly win or even survive. There is a plan here, and the details are starting to come out *en masse*, thanks again to the dedication of parents, teachers, citizens, and students who want answers. Now, they are wanting more than answers. They want action. That is what this book is all about.

The only feasible response to this top-down Federal and corporate takeover is bottom-up revolution and resistance. Many groups and protesters have become part of this response, and this is truly what grassroots looks like. This is a relatively small collection of some of their stories. When everyone and everything we are supposed to trust seem signed on to the mandates from the few at the top, the many at the bottom can find no allies there. We look to each other and we organize.

This book seeks to arm parents, teachers, students, and citizens with the background knowledge and ideas for action that will activate them into the roles we need them to take on.

This book will also offer some successes and setbacks that the movement to reclaim our schools has already seen. I want to see every parent of school-aged children taking to the streets, the boardrooms, the statehouses, the assemblies, the PTAs, and the voting booths ready to fight for their kids. That is how we will win. That is how the people of the United States will reclaim their coveted public education system, as well as so much more. Apathy and inaction will lead us rapidly down a path that we not only can't imagine, but certainly don't want to see. Let this be our call to action. Let's save our kids. Let's save our country.

INTRODUCTION

I'm just going to cut to the chase, and then I'll use the rest of the book to discuss this basic idea and showcase the fight against it:

The goal of the education reform movement in the United States, under Race to the Top and No Child Left Behind, is to manufacture and propagandize a crisis—the failure of the public school system—and use the response to that crisis to sell corporate education wares, lead this next generation down a pre-chosen path toward career training, and maintain corporate dominance in the global economy.

It sounds crazy, I know. I hope to use the remaining pages to show why it's not crazy, and what the growing grassroots movements of parents, teachers, citizens, and even students are doing to stop it from ruining our schools and, ultimately, our kids' futures. Let start this off with a little bit of social engineering history.

In 2009, when the concerted effort to blast teachers for the economic (and other) woes of the cities and states that supported them went mainstream, I had to do a double-take at the things that were being pressed in the media. It became trendy, all of a sudden, to blame teachers for everything from low test scores to local economic failures, from child behavior problems to losing American jobs to India and China, from local crime problems to bad parenting. The media became temporarily addicted to shaming and spotlighting teachers. And their unions. It was a fallacy to lump together the important work that teachers do in the classrooms every day in this country and equate it with the actions that the unions take on a national level, especially when those actions were either made-up or strictly anecdotal.

The blame was severe and it was not just some scapegoat procedure that someone just happened to stumble upon. This was an orchestrated step in the big plan to remove or weaken resistance to the education reform movement that has seized this country and is bulldozing its way through public schools. We're all targets in the plan, and we've mostly bought into it as a nation (or, at best, ignored it).

If you've been paying attention, you've also realized that the division between "left" and "right" has become much more pronounced, much wider, and much more vitriolic. Labels have been exaggerated, and terms have been hijacked. One good example I can think of is the word *progressive*. A progressive person used to be someone who wanted to see things change to match the need of the times. Now, somehow, it has become a symbol of tyranny and government overreach. Many questioned my use of the word in *Children of the Core*, as I used it to describe the way education should be viewed. A progressive teacher is one who knows that children must be guided to confront problems with an open mind and a ready skillset. It has nothing to do with feeding children ideologies that prepare them to be ripe for the picking of a communist or otherwise "globally sustainable" society (another term that has taken on new meaning. There is certainly evidence for such a movement being passed among the neoliberals in government, universities, corporate America, and the world, but progressive educators generally neither associate themselves with that movement nor do they have much knowledge of it.

The word *global* is another such term. Global thinking means that a student or citizen has an understanding of the rest of the world--the needs, the thoughts, the politics, the struggles, the populations, the economics, and the movements. This is important if someone is looking to be a well-rounded and communicative member of his or her own society—the ability to think outside the borders and communicate with other nationalities is a key to success in one's own society. It does not mean that there must be a move toward some one-size-fits-all global commune where everyone gives up national rights, pride, property, or identity in exchange for "citizenship." These are terms that have been reshaped. I don't know for sure who took over their meanings, but it's a shame to see. Rewriting the language and confusing the public is one strategy for slipping bad policy past the public awareness.

Part of the plan was also to change the discourse—the ways we talk to each other about certain things and how we interact with people who are labeled differently from us. Without any evidence or background, we are told to distrust certain people, hate people different from us, make assumptions about their intentions, remove ourselves from their discussions (or attempt to forcefully try to change their minds), and never, ever agree with anything they say, simply based on their labels. Realistically, nobody is afforded all the blame and nobody is blameless, and this is certainly nothing new (the overall public discourse has steadily become more venomous since the 1980s). The whole idea of poisoning the discourse is to build and maintain perpetual tension in American society. Why, for the love of creation, would anyone want to do that? Here's why:

It is the best distraction technique known to humans.

Keep them fighting about things that are hawked as important (most of them aren't that critical) and they will ignore what's happening behind their backs. Like I said, none of us can escape the blame, but we were (and are) being played like pawns in a board game. The "us versus them" mentality is epidemic in this country and it's been our greatest weakness. Left vs. right, conservative vs. liberal, this religion vs. that religion, Democrat vs. Republican, etc. It's mind-boggling, it's well orchestrated by those who wish to keep us distracted, and it's constantly streamed to us via various media sources. *Constantly.*

Something interesting happens when the population is divided by issues of varying degrees of importance. The division itself becomes all-encompassing and redirects our attention and vigilance towards the perceived problems or threats or bogeymen, which we start to believe are caused by the group of people on the other side. I've lost count of how many times I've heard a self-proclaimed liberal warn everyone on the Internet of the horrible things that conservatives are plotting in order to destroy our way of life. I've also lost count of how many times I've heard a self-proclaimed conservative say the exact same thing about liberals.

There's hardly ever any real evidence, other than some legislator or other leader spouting something that he or she knows will get people foaming at the mouth. In most cases, no action is ever taken by that leader, but that's not the point anyway. The point is to get the polarity back where it's wanted. The point is to get the two sides moving farther apart and back to bickering. When a line is drawn in the sand, even for relatively trivial issues, and the American public is told to choose on which side they will stand, a poisonous discourse is created. One side calls the other treasonous, those who stand in the middle are weak and indecisive, while the true criminals and traitors crawl silently along the sidelines—out of sight and out of mind.

And this is how it's done. This is how very serious, very big, and very dangerous ideas and mandates are pushed under the people's radars and into our lives without us even knowing it. We are bombarded with "problems," which we are told require our immediate and focused attention. We are told what horrible and asinine things "they" are doing and what we need to do to stop it. In many cases, "they" are our own neighbors and friends. And in most cases, the "problems" aren't problems.

Introduction

A smart gentleman told me recently, when you are in charge of a military, and you have just one skirmish to deal with, you send your troops to deal with that problem. When you have fifty skirmishes, you have to do some triage to determine the most critical course of action, which is difficult. I would argue that it's even more difficult in civilian life, when the most challenging part of that process is the triage. We can't seem to agree what needs the most attention right now, since the media and their propaganda show several issues at once as being severe. And they tend to leave out the actions that require our most immediate attention and are most critical. Big skirmishes that will cost us the bigger "war" are not discussed with the public. It is my contention that the most dangerous skirmish the American people are ignoring right now is the education privatization movement. I made sound biased, but I hope to convince my readers by the time they finish this book.

American media and more politically-tuned citizens were so busy arguing about everything else during the 2008 election, nobody even thought to ask where No Child Left Behind was going or what was next. It was largely ignored, as education often is during intense political battles. I can see why. People were losing houses, jobs, and livelihoods. We were arguing over whether we should save the banks or let them die. We were wondering if we should save car manufacturers or let them die. We were debating over the apparent future of our very economy. And, then, of course, we were bickering about homosexuals getting married, Mexican immigrants stealing jobs, and who is doing a better job of ignoring the poor troops sacrificing in our two quagmires in the Middle East. Who had time to talk about education?

So, we didn't talk about it. We allowed the newly elected president and his education secretary to take the reins and lead us down whatever path they chose. We trusted them. They gave us the product of years of planning and scheming. They gave us Race to the Top.

Not too long ago, I suggested that the Common Core and Race to the Top spell the end of American Exceptionalism because of the way they portend to educate our next generation. I heard recently from a strong educator that it isn't necessary to be number one in the world, because, what's the point? And number one at what, exactly? I agree with both of those responses, but that's not what I'd meant.

The response likely comes from the deluge of reprimands that we're used to hearing from those who wish to buy the American education system. According to the international tests scores from the Program for International Student Assessment (PISA) and Trends in International Mathematics and Science Study (TIMSS), we are certainly not number one in the world in test scores. There has been a major campaign in the media, fed by several sources, stating: if we don't start seeing those test scores go up, we are going to sink into a terrible economic slump and we will not survive the economic booms of countries like China, Japan, Indonesia, India, or the conglomerate European Union. This media storm has been the necessary (and apparently successful) move to allow corporate giants, politicians, and other education reformers to inject their agendas and goals into the education policy discussion by discrediting everything about the *status quo*. First, it was bad teachers, then the unions that protect them, and now, the university programs that prepare them.

Failing schools, bad parenting, bad state and district policies, not having enough rigor and relevance in our schools, and--most recently--poor teacher preparation programs are all part of the blame game for why our international test scores aren't better than everyone else. The next chapter will introduce the major players of that smear movement, what they advertise as their motives, and what they have been doing or will do about it.

Race to the Top (RttT) was touted publicly as the best way to use American Recovery and Reinvestment Act (ARRA) dollars to fund and improve schools. Instead of using distribution models based on income, ZIP code, disabilities, or other historical bases, RttT was a competitive model. States and districts that wanted to receive this new Federal funding (and, let's face it, after the state budget crises in 2008 and later, *every* state needed money from the Feds) were required to participate in a lengthy application process, in which they promised the U.S. Department of Education to try everything in their power to improve their public schools. And by "improve," I mean cling to the promises to close achievement gaps, show consistent student achievement growth among all subgroups, and increase proficiency rates—all based on standardized summative tests.

Basically, in order to qualify for funds, there were five main things that states and districts had to plan in detail and promise to do:

1. Show that the entire state is committed to the entire reform plan that is being used in the application process;

2. Adopt common standards and methods of common assessments (and participate in a consortium of "a significant number of states" that are doing the same);

3. Create and use a "comprehensive" state longitudinal data system to track student growth and achievement and improve instruction;

4. Create a plan to recruit and retain "effective" teachers and leaders, evaluate them based on student achievement, and support or remove teachers who are not effective; and

5. Turn around low-performing schools.[9]

States invested many hours and plenty of money to put together these applications, often with the help and advice of reform groups that were pushing down the door for the opportunities to put their influence and names on the application or supporting documents. Competing for money is what corporations do, so it makes sense that their nonprofits and "philanthropy foundations" would more than happy to help. After all, many of the things in that list of 5 have *investment opportunity* written all over them.

This book will look more closely at each of these items more closely as we move through it, and will help shed some light on how the realities of those plans are playing out in cities and states around the country, and how it's affecting kids of all ages and backgrounds.

The purpose of *Uncommon*, however, is to shine a spotlight on the people and the movements that no one ever hears about, since the corporate media is mostly a mouthpiece of the reform movement. In 2009, teachers and education experts started to criticize Race to the Top as a way to make No Child Left Behind (NCLB) worse. Not only was the Federal government still requiring schools to meet Adequate Yearly Progress (AYP), but now schools were being required to buy in to common standards and assessments as the rest of the state, and states were required to join consortia of states in order to receive money.

Arne Duncan stated that his new program was a way to end the one-size-fits-all requirements of NCLB, and that RttT would bring American students back into a system that provides "rigor and relevance," and prepare them for 21st century colleges and careers. He even offered a waiver procedure to get out of the NCLB requirements, with the understanding that waived states would meet the demands of the Race to the Top[10]. The phrase, "out of the frying pan and into the fire," comes to mind.

Teachers, for large part, didn't buy it. Many of us referred to it as "NCLB on steroids," given its tendency to adopt the same methods and consequences as the old law, yet more stringently and severely. Right away, teachers endured hours of "professional development" that showed us that we've been doing this wrong the whole time. Some training was good, and even applicable to our grade levels and content, but much of it showed that district administration was just as confused and skeptical as the rest of us.

Of course, there are teachers who tend to laser-focus on the standards they teach, without paying much attention to what's happening before or after their class. They also tend to try to stay out of the arguments about testing, data collection, narrowed curriculum, setting kids and schools up for failure, and the eventual loss of their very jobs. While I do understand the propensity to remain "under the radar" or defiantly in the classroom doing what's best for kids, regardless of what the top brass says, I do not understand the idea of a professional teacher buying into all of this with acceptance and compliance and without evidence or research.

As early as 2010, conservative groups such as The Heritage Foundation, The American Principles Project, The Pioneer Institute, and others have been trying to get a message out that the Common Core State Standards were not what they appeared to be. Perhaps partisanship and the aforementioned cynicism with which we were conditioned played a part, but those groups were largely ignored. After all, this was an Obama Administration initiative, and we would all expect conservative think tanks to disavow anything put in place by that administration. Regardless, the videos and reports put out were largely valid, if slightly alarmist. However, some are outright incorrect. I will speak more about those groups in the last chapter of the book, and my hopes for the near future.

Introduction

I'm often asked about my affiliations, my political leanings, and my feelings about other issues. First, there is no other issue right now for me. I feel a sense of urgency about the course of public education in this country, and I believe that every other issue facing us relies on its outcomes. Also, I'm not a member of any political party and I refuse to be labeled as liberal or conservative, since I'm liberal concerning some issues and conservative regarding others. (That's apparently another no-no in this country.) I am a parent, an educator, and an American who lives in an increasingly global society.

I see lots of partisan and ideological fingerpointing in education discussions. I want to share the things I've learned about all of this, with the hopes of easing up on the divisiveness. You see, partisanship is just another distraction. The movement to save our kids and their schools is too important for distractions.

The education "reform" movement was spearheaded by the likes of Arne Duncan, Democrats for Education Reform (DFER), Michelle Rhee, Bill Gates, and other notable names in the news—people who proclaim themselves as Democrats. Following their work and loving every minute of it are such notable names as Jeb Bush, Rupert Murdoch, Chris Christie, Tony Bennett, and (arguably) Mitt Romney, who proclaim themselves as Republicans.

So, here's what we have to deal with: the reform movement that is dismantling our public schools is a firmly bipartisan nightmare. That's because party politics have very little to do with this. It's all about the Benjamins.

Introduction

The current uprising we're seeing among parents, teachers, and students is motivating and inspirational. Well, most of the time. You see, what caused parents to wake up and start boycotting standardized tests and the Common Core State Standards had nothing to do with partisan politics. Actually, it had nothing to do with politics at all. It came about because parents love their kids. When our kids are suffering in any way, we take action to stop that suffering. (I reminded New York Education Commissioner John King about this recently[11].) Our motivations don't come from our stances on other issues.

However, a deeper look into what's happening also makes a lot of us realize that our own kids aren't the only stakes in this game. We also are coming around to the idea that the future of our country is at stake. I hope that this is going to open the doors to a new, larger public movement. We are now waking up to the realities of living under common national education standards, corporate data mining, and specialized "niche" learning. And this is where we really need to start to come together.

I've seen a lot of folks try to equate this issue with several other issues around us, which all apparently have a left vs. right or liberal vs. conservative or Democrat vs. Republican vibe to them. This is not an issue that can be divided along those lines. This is an issue that has no lines drawn in the sand or political parties to blame.

Here are a few points to consider:

This is not a *progressive* agenda. I am a progressive educator—meaning I believe that the world is changing too fast to be using Industrial Age techniques to teach Information Age kids. I understand that there is talk of a progressive movement, which seeks to globalize all peoples of all nations in order to create a sustainable future for the planet. This talk seems to me to be another division technique used by the corporate elite behind economic and education reform, since they were the target of the previous progressive movement at the turn of the 20th century. Whether global sustainability is beneficial or damning is an issue that will continue to be debated. But progressive educators and progressive education are different. Just because the "reformers" call themselves Democrats doesn't mean they are progressive, in any sense of the word. They are corporate puppets, stooges, and panderers.

This is not a *conservative* agenda. I am also a conservative educator—meaning I do not believe that public education should be changed to become a Federal and nationalized system. Again, corporations are not automatically conservative. They aren't anything other than self-serving and profit-minded. And education policy should be advised and led by educators, not politicians or corporations. In other words, we need to fix what's ailing the specific schools that aren't holding their own within the system; we don't need to overhaul the entire system to fix less than 10% of schools.

This is not *socialism* or *communism*. Those two terms refer to the means of production and resources being either controlled or taken over by the state and distributed as equally as possible. This has been stated, along with the "progressive" thing, as the goal of globalists: to seize control of private property and wealth and start distributing it more evenly among all peoples of the planet. That's not what's happening with education. This "reform" movement is corporate-run, with the government in partnership. Common Core does not equal communism.

This is not *fascism*, although it does come very close. Fascism generally refers to extreme nationalism and the totalitarianism that comes with it. America teeters dangerously close to this type of system, with patriotism and religion as the go to strategies to get people to fall in line with a given mandate or top-down initiative. I haven't seen anyone equate over-the-top American pride with the Common Core State Standards, especially since it was basically sneaked past us before we knew about it; however, it is most certainly an attempt by the wealthy and the corporations to seize control of the means of education and, therefore, production. And this isn't Nazism. If it were, then the government would have taken over the corporations in order to serve its own purposes. If anything, we're seeing the reverse. This reform belongs in its own category of fascist-like control: *corporatism*.

This has nothing to do with *redistribution of wealth* from the rich to the poor. No wealth is being redistributed to the poor, other than the grants and contributions of billionaires and corporations in support of the privatization of schools for their own purposes. The danger we're seeing is the continued increases in tax dollars on the middle class to fund corporate takeovers of school districts and school buildings and the expensive

Introduction

of Common Core and high-stakes testing

This is, absolutely, a means for *indoctrination*. But not for or against any ideology, religion, or political party (although we've started to see more of those materials released in individual states). This is how wealthy corporate owners and investors get to secure their own future—by setting our kids up to serve their place in it. Our kids are being indoctrinated with the values of menial and repetitive work. They are being trained to sit in cubicles, not to follow their dreams.

I want to emphasize that last point. This is a corporate agenda. This is the planning and preparation stage for the America that has been dreamed up by CEOs and other assorted moneybags who have not a shred of national pride or sense of community. This also isn't just about a $500 billion industry known as public education; this is about the future!

This is unprecedented and never before seen in our country. Our corporate leaders, our billionaires, and most of our government leaders have become equal partners in this takeover. Their kids are secure in their futures, as they will grow to take their places among the movers and the shakers and the innovators and the owners in the United States.

The rest of us? Well, our kids have futures that are guided based on what they can accomplish against the national standards in place in 45 states, the tests that are measuring their standardized skills, and the data tracking that will determine their best course of study and work.

And if you think those national standards promise that every kid will be ready to be successful in 21st century America, you need to ask yourself what "successful" means in that context. It's taking on a very different meaning than what we're used to hearing.

Parents, unfortunately, really had no idea what was happening, and I believe that was by design. Parents tend to ask a lot of questions, especially about things happening with their kids; things that they've never heard of. There were some trickle-down rumors coming from schools regarding some "race to the top" thing, and new rigor, and good stuff for kids. At around the same time the word was slowly moving through parent circles, President Obama got on the television and told kids that they need to step up and study and work hard in school. In some sense, the things he said were true and probably answered problems in the lives of several million children. But the timing was strange, and the poignancy of a national leader telling young kids to get ready and start doing a better job in school was a little strange. And, once again, it caused a rift in parent opinion and action. Some cooed and were grateful for being such a caring leader; others seethed and were offended by the idea that parents can't do that on their own. Others, like me, tilted our heads in curiosity and wondered what the president's angle was.

I'm convinced it was another distraction strategy, but also a strategy to get some parents to become hyper-involved. First, when you get busy or uninvolved parents to look more deeply at their kids, you can get them to feel defensive and guilty at the same time: "I know he's not talking about *me*; but just in case, I'm going to start upping my game." Or, you just plain offend the parents who don't believe that the Federal government has any place in the living room, telling parents what to do. "I do everything right for my kids! Who does he think he is?" When parents like the latter are put on the offensive, they tend to start observing and asking about details. Either way, the impact is generally the same for all parents.

For one thing, the message was meant to get all parents on board to help kids become better prepared and stronger people in preparation for the challenging times ahead. It was also an attempt to get kids to start gearing themselves up for the changes to come. School personnel were directed to start working more on strict discipline, bell-to-bell work periods, and keeping kids constantly on task. Real school reform doesn't allow for daydreaming, socializing, or other shenanigans. Some parents questioned the changes to the school day, but were usually eased by the reassuring words of principals and teachers that this is leading to something great.

One thing that started to come into vogue at about this time was a whole new level of public school bashing, which inaugurated and benchmarked by the film, *Waiting for Superman*, and plugged relentlessly by StudentsFirst founder, Michelle Rhee, and other supporters of charter school takeovers. When parents are told to take a closer look at everything in their kids' lives, at the same time that national talking heads are screaming about failing schools, the corpor

that parents will call for "better" schools. '

will be waiting with fake concern, as well a̲

trigger" legislation or vouchers or something of the sort,

rid those parents of those terrible, awful, mean, ol' schools anᴅ

replace them with shiny, new charter schools. And they'll even offer to get rid of those whiny, overpaid veteran teachers and replace them with brand-new, young, enthusiastic, Teach for America temps.

Groups like Parent Revolution (which is not made up of parents), StudentsFirst, Great Schools, the Walton Foundation and the Eli and Edythe Broad Foundation, lobbied for parent support to pass laws or rally to improve school conditions. The American Legislative Exchange Council (ALEC) was happy to start writing model bills in support of that lobbying. In select cases, there actually are severe problems with the schools or districts, and action needs to be taken. However, most parents who pulled the "parent trigger" found themselves regretting the decision, since it's not the solution they were looking for, and they found themselves unable to back out. That's because, as I'll discuss more later, these organizations (known as "astroturfers") are not grassroots organizations that have the best interest of children at the center of their campaigns. They are lobbying groups that have their corporate clients' interests at heart.

It's true that several of these groups have either operated as, or have been labeled as Republican constructs. Obviously, Republicans do not represent the entirety of education reform,

one of the most active astroturf organizations is named
mocrats for Education Reform, and Michelle Rhee is a self-
proclaimed Democrat.

It's taking Democrats and other Obama supporters a little
longer to start questioning and understanding what's happening.
For one thing, Obama ran on a campaign of "hope and change" in
2008, and that meant to most of his supporters that he could help
lead them into a brighter future for their children. Fancy talking
points like quality education for every child, bright future for every
child, and jobs of the future for every child rang beautiful in
parents' ears. Now that the reality is starting to drown that ring,
supporters find themselves in dissonance. They loved Obama—
they still want to—but they sense something isn't right.

With more and more information coming to light, there has
been an underground movement brewing and growing to counter
the dangerous and overwhelming moves by corporate and
government reformers. Underground isn't where this grassroots
movement wants to dwell, but the media isn't grabbing it and
many parents and teachers are living and working in fear of the
implications and consequences of speaking out. Several teachers
have been warned, chastised, suspended, fired, or have left of their
own necessity. The teachers' union representation is absent when
needed the most or, worse, on board with the reform agenda.

Parents continue to show they are fearless, but are still
bogged down by the threats of state education departments
against them and their children. Students are trapped in the thick
of it all, feeling the pressure from above and wary of speaking out

to those of whom they are raised to be respectful and obedient. Even school and district administrators are stuck with the weight of delivering Federal and state mandates under threat of being shown the door.

There are heroes among all of them. I will tell their stories and their successes in part two.

I believe this is the one issue of the day that will begin to blur or delete party lines, ideological polarizations, and labels among American citizens. This is the one issue of the times that will make people stop wearing their labels on their sleeves--conservative, liberal, Republican, Democrat, Independent, Christian, atheist, Jewish, Muslim, etc.--and start realizing that this is a very large, deeply embedded problem that is attacking our most precious gifts: *our children.*

I also fear that the growth of corporate power and wealth is blurring and deleting party lines in our government. America has always teetered dangerously close to transforming into a totalitarian state, since we only have two active and powerful political parties. The current merger of Republicans, Democrats, and large corporations in the education takeover of America's next generation (among other important issues) is unnerving. While the power elite continues to sell us "choice," we are quickly finding that there is a rapid decrease in choice--in just about everything of real value.

A very wise and active mother once spoke to a large crowd of people with some words, which always come to mind when I see people trapped in planned and poisonous discourse. Sometimes they fight about guns. Sometimes they fight about food stamps. Sometimes they fight with others just for being someone other than who they are. Sometimes, I offer that parent's words to those poor folks:

There are many, many issues—some of them important and near and dear to us—that may affect our kids as they grow and may affect the future in which they grow. But, there is only one issue facing our nation today that will truly shape that future and ultimately change the face of the nation in which our kids grow. That issue is education. The government and corporate takeover is, by far, the most important challenge our nation faces today, and it is the responsibility of 'We the People' to fight back and secure our children's future hopes and dreams.

There's room for hope. Parents around the country, along with the teachers who bravely speak out, are putting aside superficial differences to join in this most important struggle. Throughout this book, I hope to present the facts, evidence, and connections that make us more aware of the bigger picture surrounding the nonsense, and start to focus more on the things that are truly dangerous. I will focus on the corporate and government collusion to take over public education and how dangerous that is, which has opened the eyes of many to how close we are to losing our way.

Parents love their children. Teachers love their students. A large number of the American people fit into the former category and will do whatever it takes to make sure their kids are safe and secure in their lives. We want our children to be individuals, with hopes and dreams that are always on the horizon and within their eventual reach. Different people have different challenges, but education has always remained the path to fulfillment of all potentials. When a system is designed to standardize learning, growing, developing, and becoming—and to be the only game in town—it is inherently stifling, at best, and dangerous, at worst.

So, we fight the "train that has already left the station," because we must. We are the sworn protection and guidance for these innocents and we stand in between them and that which may harm them. We are learning to look a little deeper, ask harder questions, and seek better ways to educate them. We are protesting the destruction of their schools, the ostracism of their teachers, and the insults to their parents. We are the force that will meet the top-down takeover of our world-acclaimed public education system with a bottom-up revolution. This is why we fight, how we fight, and how we will win.

PART ONE

The Face of the Enemy

CHAPTER

1

Race to the Top

In December 2008, after winning the national election, President-elect Barack Obama chose the former CEO of Chicago Public Schools, Arne Duncan, to run his Department of Education. Most of the mainstream media heralded the choice, based on successes that were perceived (or real) in the Chicago system under Duncan's leadership. Proficiency rates in Chicago schools, based on test scores, had increased from 38 to 67 percent, and dropout rates had decreased dramatically while Duncan was in charge. The validity of these increases is *still* being debated, and the successes that are verifiable are often claimed to have happened *in spite* of Duncan's leadership.

Teachers and other educational stakeholders weren't as happy about Obama's choice, since Arne Duncan did not come from an education background. Almost from the beginning, social media groups started to spring up, asking President Obama to reconsider the choice and to replace Mr. Duncan with someone who knows what he or she is talking about. Robert Valiant's Dump Duncan[12] group on Facebook is perhaps the oldest and most active, with almost 2,000 members and a petition that has traveled the world many times and has been submitted to the White House asking for Duncan's dismissal. Interestingly, Mr. Obama passed up the well-known education researcher, Linda Darling-Hammond, for the position. I still wonder how things might have been different if she had been assigned the post.

I want to talk a little about what Race to the Top was supposed to accomplish, how it was sold, and how the deal of the decade has set the stage for educational failure and dysfunction in our nation's schools.

On Your Marks, Get Set...

The White House website offers the summary of what Obama and Duncan wanted the American public to think[13]:

> Race to the Top marks a historic moment in American education. This initiative offers bold incentives to states willing to spur systemic reform to improve teaching and learning in America's schools. Race to the Top has ushered in significant change in our education system, particularly in raising standards and aligning policies and structures to the goal of college and career readiness. Race to the Top has helped drive states nationwide to pursue higher standards, improve teacher effectiveness, use data

effectively in the classroom, and adopt new strategies to help struggling schools.

The program was sold as a way to offer "bold incentives" to states and districts that signed onto and followed the requirements of the initiative and modeled "innovative" practices that led to higher student achievement. These bold incentives were nothing more than cash for cash-strapped state education departments. The innovative ways of thinking and teaching were nothing more than preset requirements that had to be met in order to receive that badly needed funding. In short, the Federal Department of Education had prepared a competition that relied on the desperation of our schools to ensure participation. Race to the Top is a bribe. Pure and simple.

This program is incredibly misguided. Bribes and competition may be effective strategies in the corporate world, after which RttT is modeled, but it takes a little more than that to gain acceptance by parents, educators, and citizens who think more deeply than the business-minded surface of education. So, with the help of the many friends you'll read about in the next chapter, the Department of Education and the White House got busy plugging the deal. In order to bring everyone on board, a tried-and-true method—older than Arne himself—was employed: let's use the media to scare the hell out of everyone by saying that *we are all doomed and will soon be speaking Chinese because our education system is so bad that our next generation will find itself serving as the labor force for some Eastern megacorporation and, oh my god, it's the end of America!*

The best way to sell a product that has questionable value and will likely be rejected by the majority of *thinking* people is to make them believe that they must have it to ensure their own survival. Or, at least, their continued comfort. The other way to ensure that a program this suspect gets accepted is to convince the public that they really don't need to do anything, other than maybe help kids with their homework, buy some educational products for the home computer, and just let the experts in Washington and scattered think tanks do the hard work.

Oh, and parents, be ready to scrutinize your kids' schools. If they aren't towing the line in this important "race," you need to speak up.

I spent plenty of time discussing how Race to the Top came into play, what the background was, and how it was put into practice in *Children of the Core*. Let's spend a little quality time looking more closely at the talking points that are being spread like wildfire to promote the program, followed by some reality discussion. Most of these are related the Common Core State Standards (CCSS), which are an integral part of RttT, and which I claim are the bedrock upon which everything else sits.

Let's start with a multiple-choice test question. What was the most effective talking point that Arne Duncan used to put Race to the Top into play so quickly and easily? Choose the best answer:

A. Everybody's Doing it

In almost every article and almost every video about the Common Core Standards, you will see that 46 states, plus the District of Columbia, have adopted those standards. This tidbit is almost always in the first couple of sentences of the material being presented, so it must be something that promoters consider very important to the viewers, readers, or listeners. I'm not sure why those who promote this brand of reform resort to using a logical fallacy in order to convince people that the standards are good for us. The "bandwagon" fallacy attempts to validate something based on its popularity, and it's used widely in this scenario.

Unfortunately, there is no way to validate a set of content standards based on the fact that almost every state has adopted and are currently implementing them (especially since several states are seeking ways to withdraw their decisions, after having the chance to actually see and work with them). Basically, these states had no choice: adopting common standards (and joining a consortium of states that are doing the same) was part of the deal. That's part of the bribe. Dangling a cash carrot in front of the states, watching the majority of them take the bait, and then saying that the standards are thus valid is highly disingenuous and completely fallacious.

What many people still don't realize is that most states didn't win grant money from Race to the Top to pay for the changes and the implementations. In order to qualify, states had to show their timelines for putting into place the standards, testing programs, and teacher evaluation plans, along with the strategies and commitments to do so. In phase one of the competition, which was apparently nothing more than a practice run, only two states won a small amount of money. The Department of Education gave feedback to the states that didn't win (read: didn't quite match up to the narrow guidelines of "innovative" changes laid out by the Department) so that they could be more competitive in the next round.

Phase two was the big one, and states spent more resources to revise their applications in order to qualify and boost their competitiveness for the next round of payouts. This time around, ten states received prizes of various amounts for "winning" the contest. So far, only 12 states, out of the 46 that applied, have won Federal grants from Arne's Education Department[14]. The question that many have asked in the circles in which I spend my time is: Why did the losing states still continue with adoption of the Common Core State Standards and the initiation into testing consortia, even without the prize money that was supposed to pay for it?

Finally, in an attempt to solidify commitments from more local environments, phase three of RttT (the district competition) chose 16 winning applications (out of 372) in 11 states[15].

Even in the losing states and districts, Arne Duncan stated, the program was boosting the innovations that he required. He heralded RttT as a program that has a ripple effect, as the winners of the grant money were influencing the schools that didn't win. Perhaps this is true. Perhaps the ripple effect followed the fallacy. Everybody's doing it; if we don't jump on the bandwagon, we may lose opportunities for funding or materials or respect or whatever else comes down the pipe. Perhaps with some districts, there was real buy-in and belief in the Common Core and the testing that is aligned to it. Perhaps the knowledge of the entire system wasn't well understood. I believe the circumstances are different for every state and district. That's why we see opposition from some and complete faith in others.

B. Common Standards Keep Mobile Kids Caught Up

Right away, let me suggest that this is not an adequate justification for a national set of common standards and a complete rewrite of the way education works in this country. Let me also add that this does not qualify as a crisis in America. The hardships of student mobility exist for about 15 percent of students from Kindergarten through eighth grade, and the majority of that 15 percent are poor, minority, or single-parent households, with another 13 percent of mobile students living in military households. Only 2% of K-12 students actually move across state lines during that 13-year span. Again, we see the educational policymakers trying to find a way around dealing with another measurement of poverty, without actually taking a good look at the effects of poverty on student mobility, as well as many other things.

The National Center for Educational Accountability has suggested that longitudinal student databases be developed to track mobile students for better placement based on academic needs. The NCEA states that, in order for that to be effective, a common national curriculum would need to be implemented nationwide and statewide student identification programs would need to be enacted to monitor student movements. This is speculation, however, and has many critics of its efficacy, its necessity, and its true mission. It should also be noted that NCEA is funded and advised by the ACT Corporation, which I will talk about in a few pages[16].

I also wish that this was a sincere concern for the Department of Education, the Common Core State Standards Initiative, or any other policy body. The fact is, this is a justification after the fact. Just another "perk" to add in selling standards and ideas that have no significant research base or history of field testing. There is also no empirical evidence that common standards or student databases would alleviate the effects of frequent school changes.

What has worked in the past are relatively simple and low-tech idea that have been shown empirically to work: student buddy systems, professional development for teachers in high-mobility areas, and providing outreach programs to parents to help minimize the effects of frequent mobility. In summary, high mobility for a very small portion of students does not warrant a nationwide collusion of common standards, common curricula, common assessments, and longitudinal student tracking—especially when there is no evidence to suggest success.

One more time: to justify a national gamble, based on no pilots, field tests, or other meaningful evidence, is simply bad policy. To say that student mobility is a good reason to standardized our nation's schools is short-sighted and incredibly naïve, especially since there's no evidence at all to suggest that Common Core Standards will alleviate the generally minor problems that accompany those students. This is 15% of the K-12 population, of which 85% are living at or below the poverty line. This justification is simply another way to keep from looking at the real problems in American life. Even the Government Accountability Office recognized that poverty plays a part in the difficulties of school changes, and that poverty is usually accountable for the relocations in the first place[17]. That research has been conveniently ignored.

C. Race to the Top Prepares Students to Compete in the Global Economy

Arne Duncan believes that his Race to the Top program will come together in a magical way to prepare all of the children of the United States for the 21st century as competitive members of the global society. He and his boss have been heard to say that this is a revolutionary time in American education, when we finally create bold new initiatives and innovative programs to lead our children to success.

The foundation of the Obama Administration's education reform is undoubtedly the Common Core State Standards, the product of a consortium of private trade groups, which worked for a few years to bring to fruition the vision laid out by Bill Gates and other commission sources, as well as the global ideals brought forth by "progressive" Democrats and corporate elites. The standards were created using a backwards-mapping method, which means that a model of an ideal high school graduate, with ideal sets of content knowledge, was created among members of the National Governors Association (NGA) and the Council of Chief State School Officers (CCSSO). The process needed to create that perfect graduation candidate was the job of Achieve, Inc., a private, nonprofit company which the NGA and the CCSSO partnered with in order to legally influence and lobby education policy.

One of their most important reasons for creating the Common Core Standards, they will tell us, is to make sure that students are prepared for college and career and to be prepared to compete globally. Another line you can find in just about every, single document about the Common Core is the one about them being "internationally benchmarked" against the best standards in the world. This benchmarking is incredibly vague and is outlined in a document titled, "Benchmarking for Success: Ensuring U.S. Students Receive a World-Class Education[18]." There a few specific examples, such as the idea that top-performing countries have 8th graders doing algebra and geometry, while most American 8th graders are still doing arithmetic.

Actually, most American math classes offer two or more choices, based on readiness and preparation. Yes, most American kids are doing arithmetic in 8th grade—although it has been traditional to call it pre-algebra—but there are large numbers of students in 8th grade who do take what we call Algebra I, and receive high school credit for it. Honestly, I have a hard time understanding why that's a bad thing, much less a national crisis.

Another example states that while 8th grade kids in other countries are learning how the eye works in certain animals, American kids are learning to name the parts of the eye. I, having read science curricula from several states, having taught 8th grade life science, and having observed several science classrooms over the years, will go ahead and call this a lie, or at least a generalization based on very little evidence.

It wasn't too long ago that I was browsing the FAQ section of the CCSSI website and noticed that the question regarding international benchmarking had a new answer. The new answer stated that the CCSS were internationally "influenced." A month later, I visited the FAQ again, and the benchmarking claim had returned. It seems difficult to make up one's mind when the original claims are based on shoddy research and non-existent evidence.

As Chris Tienken eloquently states, there is no empirical evidence that common national content standards and very high scores on international tests in K-12 has any effect on national economies. There is simply no correlation. If there were, we would see the economies of Finland, Singapore, and South Korea (to name a few) continue to grow rapidly. Actually, we don't see that, and neither do those nations, which is one of the reasons that several of those at the top of the achievement spectrum are beginning to abandon their "test culture" in exchange for education systems that are modeled after the American model of the 1980s and 90s. These "high-achieving" nations are actually beginning to see a slowdown in their economies due to the fact that their education systems do a poor job of graduating top scientists and engineers, entrepreneurs, and the type of collaborative, innovative and breakthrough thinking that the changing world demands[19].

Which begs the question: if top-performing countries are recently insistent on adopting and adapting the old American educational model of the turn of the millennium, why is it that America insists on jettisoning that model and adopting old, failed Asian and Eastern European national models?

D. Race to the Top Seeks to Prepare All Kids for College and Career

If I had a ten-dollar bill fall into my hands every time I read or heard "college and career," I would take my wife and kids on a very nice vacation. This phrase is used so often and with such automated reaction, it is starting to sound like there's nothing else to discuss. Why do we need Common Core? College and career. Why do we need to sign on to testing consortium that are quite expensive and are squeezing programs out of our schools? College and career. Why am I being threatened for allowing my child to opt out of standardized tests? You're ruining his chances for success in college and career. Why are we extending the school days and years? College and career. Why are you taking away my daughter's music class and replacing it with extra math classes? College and career. What's your favorite color, Mr. Duncan? Whatever color represents college and career readiness, probably.

Seriously, this is the go-to phrase of the entire process and the most overused response to every question that has been asked about Race to the Top, Common Core, national assessment consortia, charter school takeovers, and anything else having to do with education "reform." What's really frustrating is the phrase has no meaningful or true definition. What *does* "college and career ready" look like?

In 2008, during a congressional hearing regarding the reauthorization of the No Child Left Behind law, Cynthia Schmeiser, the Education Division president and chief operating officer of ACT, Inc., told lawmakers the following:

> *ACT defines college readiness as acquisition of the knowledge and skills a student needs to enroll and succeed in credit-bearing, first-year courses at a postsecondary institution, such as a two- or four-year college, trade school, or technical school...Simply stated, readiness for college means not needing to take remedial courses in postsecondary education or training programs*[20].

When Schmeiser was asked if she thought the same requirements for first-year college courses were necessary for entry-level work, she affirmed. But that doesn't make any sense. An entry-level retail associate simply doesn't need the same background knowledge and skills as an entry-level plumbing apprentice; they both start with different needed skill sets and they will both use different backgrounds to take them through their different trainings. To suggest that every student in America will need the same, static content standards to start a job or college program is not only illogical and constructed, it's also unsupported by real evidence.

The other selling point of "college and career ready" is the fact that several industrial nations are meeting or are exceeding what the ACT Corporation calls a "U.S. College and Career Ready Benchmark." ACT created this benchmark based on their own analyses, and it sits somewhere between Japan and Australia in reading, and between Switzerland and Japan in math. This is another one of Achieve's points of evidence for the Common Core State Standards being "internationally benchmarked." ACT's own analysis[21].

The problem is the same as before. There is no empirical evidence to suggest that benchmarking PISA and TIMSS scores, and meeting or exceeding those benchmarks, will have any effect on the future economy of the United States or the global competitiveness of our students in the workforce. Indeed, there are so many other factors at play in the international workforce competitiveness game, that focusing on test scores not only ignores the other factors (which is just bad science), it also supposes the conclusion before the evidence is collected (also bad science). ACT, among its kindreds, is not a research organization, by any means. They have proven themselves over and over to be little more than a propaganda and marketing firm for the corporate reform movement. They also have heavy investments in getting kids to take their array of assessments and surveys and in tracking those kids from early grades through college, in order to ensure that "students stay on target to reach their full potential throughout their educational journey." We'll talk more about this tracking and target process a little later.

Bottom line: there is simply no evidence to suggest that the Common Core State Standards, the common tests aligned to the standards, the teacher evaluations based on those test scores, or raising scores on international tests will prepare our kids to be "college and career ready," or that these things will make the U.S. globally competitive. In fact, Singapore, China, South Korea, and several European countries are looking our educational system prior to 2002 as the key to economic success and are currently working to copy it and implement it for their own cultural and national needs.

In 2009, the Education Minister of Singapore, after seeing TIMSS scores in the top 3, was asked by a reporter: *Why does Singapore always score so well on international tests, but hardly produces any top scientists or inventors?* The Minister replied that Singapore is an exam meritocracy, where America is a talent meritocracy. America doesn't just reward things that can be measured on a test, they reward things that you can't test, like creativity, innovation, collaboration, and open thinking. This is how inventors and scientists and entrepreneurs are made.

He then said that Singapore can learn a lot from America[22].

The next year, the United States released the Common Core State Standards and the Race to the Top grants, making sure that we turn our envied education system completely upside down.

That's okay, though, because this isn't about students. This is about corporations. This isn't about kids growing up prepared for the future. This is about growing a cheap labor force so that *corporations* can remain competitive (read: pulling in record profits and remaining powerful) in the global market.

So far, Race to the Top and all of its components are signaling a fear that everyone seems to disagree about: redistribution of wealth. For the past 14 years, or so, almost every major economic, healthcare, or education policy has done just that. The elite and the media keep yelling that wealth is being distributed from the "haves" to the "have-nots." At several points, polls have shown that close to half of our citizens believe that myth. The evidence, however, paints an entirely different reality: the Bush tax cuts, the Affordable Care Act, the wars in Iraq and Afghanistan, and Race to the Top are all successful methods of redistributing wealth—*to the top*. This is no accident of bad policy. The very wealthy, and the politicians who are supporting them with policy, are not concerned with the global competitiveness of American citizens. They are interested only in self-preservation and global dominance.

E. Recruiting and Retaining Great Teachers

RttT also required states to begin new teacher evaluation systems, using low-skill and low-validity assessments to measure student growth over the year and then applying those growth scores to a part of the teacher evaluation process for the year. Right away, we had problems with that. First of all, teaching common standards, using common assessments, assumes that all kids are prepared, capable, and willing to meet the exact same benchmarks at the same time. That assumption is almost as ridiculous as the NCLB goal of 100% proficiency by 2014.

Second, that process doesn't allow for variables outside of the classroom walls, such as outside activities, family income, family status, ZIP code (yes, it counts), or any other inconsistencies among same-age children. Third, it uses that imperfect quantitative measure as the make-or-break factor in a teacher's evaluation. A very well-trained and effective teacher whose students don't show growth against--let's be honest--arbitrary benchmarks is at risk of being put on developmental status, probation, or even being terminated.

In June 2013, a teacher from Douglas County School District in Colorado wrote the following post on a social media site:

> I was a teacher in DCSD this past year. I have taught, successfully, I might add, for 13 years. This year, I was informed that I would not be returning to my school as I was deemed "not a fit." That's it. No explanation, nothing more. I had my formative evaluation just one month prior, NO indication that my job was in jeopardy, nothing mentioned about areas of my teaching that may need improvement. Many of my parents were extremely upset about my not returning, and the kids were in tears, I had over 10 parents write me letters of recommendation.

In *Children of the Core*, I wrote about a Florida teacher who had been elected by her colleagues to receive the "teacher of the year" honor, which was proudly displayed outside the marquee outside of the school. At the end of the year, after factoring "value-added measures" into her annual evaluation (growth and proficiency snapshots based on standardized test scores), her overall rating was "unsatisfactory." I also spent a lot of time in the last book discussing what's wrong with these tests and why it's ridiculous and unfair to use the results as a large portion of teacher evaluations.

The fact is, "recruiting and retaining talented teachers" is increasingly looking like a euphemism for pushing out the old and quickly training the new. That's not a good thing. The veteran teachers that are leaving in droves have track records that shine above the rest and have brought success every year to many children—the kinds of success that can't be measured on standardized achievement tests. Either by early retirement, resignation, or dismissal due to low test scores (or just speaking out too much), our most needy schools are losing the best teachers. Consistently.

The reformers spin this any way they can. First, they will look at test scores, suggesting that the dismissed had to be pushed aside in order to bring in fresh, new faces that eagerly take on the challenge of "raising student achievement levels." In other words, the districts are hiring young graduates, who may or may not have a certified state teaching credential, and who more than likely came from an "alternative" teaching program, such as Teach for America. These programs have been known to use questionable data collection and reporting in order to elevate effectiveness, and their corps members generally do not last more than 2 years in the classroom before they move on to the next step in their careers.[23]

The teacher in Douglas County above did not want to leave. She was dismissed based on criteria of which she was not aware and apparently didn't meet. She didn't know one way or the other, and still doesn't. The following is the only response she's received from district leadership, from a board member who responded to her above Facebook post:

> We created this system to promote effective teacher[s] and weed out poor teachers. Sorry about your cancer, but we need great teachers in the classroom.

Sadly, this teacher also found out she had cancer prior to hearing of her discontinued employment. She also had received glowing evaluations from administration, words and letters of praise from parents, and very few and very short official observations in the classroom that counted toward her final evaluation. She was a great teacher, but not in the way that corporate reform-minded board members want her to be.

In a town near Rochester, New York, another teacher left the profession too soon, on her own terms. This was her last year teaching 3rd grade, much to the disappointment of her peers, students, parents, and administration. She saw the effects of high-stakes testing, Common Core, and the toxicity of the constant pressure of raising score as a hindrance on her professional duties and, even more distressing, on her students' happiness and progress. Coming from the same situation, I can certainly relate to her need to leave—to stop doing harm—and join the fight to save our kids and their schools. Her letter can be read later in chapter 5.

Dozens of teachers, principals, librarians, and other professionals have retired early, due to the unrealistic and punitive changes coming to schools across the nation.

So, who are these "great teachers" that the president and Michelle Rhee and state governors and the Douglas County School Board keep referring to? The temps. The corps members. The high-energy, barely trained, and score-obsessed recruits from organizations such as Teach for America, The New Teacher Project, and various other spinoffs. "Recruiting great teachers" doesn't mean what it sounds like; it should read something more like, "recruiting cheap teachers."

So, what about the "retaining" part? How do you retain a teacher that is on a two-year commitment and has better things to do with his or her time afterward? In short: you don't. That's not really a priority here. The revolving door of teachers is of no concern. Obama and his corporate friends are busy creating an army of teachers for the next decade, and where one falls, we can throw in a fresh replacement.

This is also leading to a devaluation of American school teachers. Union-busting, denying collective bargaining rights, closing "failing" schools, laying off teachers that either have lower test scores or less time on the job—it all leads to a lower paying market of education professionals. Especially when there are plenty of barely-trained temps waiting in the wings to replace those teachers. The demonization of teacher training programs as another failure opens up that domain to private takeover and further devaluing of teachers (see NCTQ in chapter 2). We've even seen prestigious education graduate program close down due to growing lack of interest in receiving master's degrees in education.[24] That's because privatization influences have convinced states to stop paying more for that credential. According to Michelle Rhee, a Teach for America temp is more effective than a veteran teacher with a master's degree (and much cheaper).

F. None of the Above

Race to the Top is the culmination of a 50-to-60-year history of wants and goals and plans for public education. The selling points are starting to wear thin, and it's becoming increasing clear that the emperor is naked (I'm *so* very sorry about the cliché; it just fits).

The Common Core State Standards, Race to the Top, the Next Generation Science Standards (NGSS), Educate to Innovate, etc.

What do all of these things have in common?

They are all, at least partially, involved with a huge movement by education reformers and politicians to boost the attention paid to science, technology, engineering, and mathematics education (STEM) in the United States. They are also the products of a highly-publicized, well-funded, and almost completely made-up crisis.

The talking points that we keep hearing in the media and from the Obama Administration are scary enough to make us think that the United States is doomed, and that the only way out of this mess is to start training a hundred thousand teachers to be super-STEM teachers, with the purpose of training more teachers in their buildings to do STEM-y stuff using prescribed curricula. That way, Obama's "Educate to Innovate" plan can become a reality: to prepare one million STEM graduates, ready to work, by 2020.[25] In a blog article, I pointed to a question about all of this:

Why? *Why* do we need one million more STEM graduates in America, when over a half of our current, well-qualified graduates can't find jobs in their chosen STEM fields? It's not because they're underqualified, and we know it. It's not because they aren't competitive against their global counterparts. It's because there simply aren't enough jobs to go around—for various reasons. So, again, why are we so involved in pushing STEM initiatives, when we actually seem to be doing okay?

One of the reasons for my question is that the United States of America isn't interested in actually investing in science or technology or engineering or mathematics for their own sakes or for the good of the people. This is evident in the following examples:

1. We don't explore space anymore,
2. We don't seem to care about the ocean floor anymore (unless there's a prospect for minerals, fuel, or other saleable materials), and
3. Our investments in redesigning, upgrading, and rebuilding our own country's infrastructure are laughable.

So, my question becomes: Why is there such a huge push for STEM education if no one is investing in any real STEM ventures, specifically ones that are working to better the lives of citizens or the understanding of our world and its place in the Universe?

It's because we don't care about any of that. The Space Shuttle fleet was recently decommissioned, due to the age of the system and the rising costs of maintenance and launch, according to Congress. Presidents George W. Bush and Barack Obama promised replacement systems, which would be revolutionary and highly utilitarian for the continuance of America's presence in space, would work to protect humans from asteroid collisions, and would push our limits to other planets. Most of the proposed programs have already been scrapped, and others have been either underfunded or put on the back burner. There is no priority here. Although the cost to build, maintain, and launch a space shuttle was roughly the same as building, maintaining, and deploying a single B-2 bomber, the priority goes to our ability to wipe foreign cities from the map. We currently rent Russian rockets to get to the International Space Station. Continued exploratory, commercial, and science missions are being left to the funds, devices, and ingenuity of private organizations, such as Space X.

NASA's budget rose slightly under Obama to fund the now-defunct Ares program. It has since seen more and more budget cuts, at the same time that the Federal government paid three times the NASA budget to Lockheed Martin, an aerospace defense corporation that visualizes space for military purposes.

So, what types of STEM projects are being bankrolled by the United States Government? Here are a few of the largest science, technology, and engineering expenditures (keep in mind that these are federal dollars being paid to private contractors):

1. Foreign-based military, relief, and nation-building operations.
2. Nuclear operations and remediation.
3. Military base support operations and technical support.
4. Military vehicles and support.
5. Pharmaceutical and Health IT companies.
6. Surveillance and reconnaissance systems and technologies.
7. Naval and aerial defense systems and machinery.
8. Missile systems and missile defense systems.

According to Achieve, Inc., the number one reason for the need of new science standards is that other countries are starting to file more patent applications with the U.S. Patent Office, bringing our percentage down, and that the United States' ranking in high-tech exports is lower than before. The second biggest reason is a debunked concern (United States students are falling behind other countries in science test score rankings). The third reason is troubling in its scope: to prepare all students for all jobs (all jobs need four years of math and science in high school, including physics and pre-calculus?). The fourth reason is to increase science literacy among American citizens. I agree with the fourth, but common content and process standards have no evidence of efficacy there.[26]

The first and third reasons for the NGSS are pretty straightforward as admissions that the real purpose of this push toward STEM for all is to maintain U.S. corporate dominance in the changing global economy. In Dora Taylor's fascinating speculation, *Empire*, it's easy to see the evidence of this.[27] The American corporate rise toward ever-increasing profits and monopoly have relied on a perpetual state of war–in one form or another–for at least 6 decades. It appears that there is a new strategy at play now. If war alone isn't promising to make the shareholders happy for very long, we need to find new ways to make strong profits off the backs of American taxpayers. And their children.

I strongly believe that large tech and energy corporations (Microsoft, General Electric, ExxonMobil, Intel, IBM, etc.) are pushing funds and propaganda into the development and spread of Common Core Standards, corporate education policies, and one-size-fits-all charter groups in order to prepare a flooded labor market to meet the corporations' needs. The results of this movement are ominous enough. But I think it's worse than that. This is an attempt to propagate the American Empire. And by American, I mean Corporate American.

By making sure that "students are globally competitive," I think we are actually seeing a move to make sure that American corporations are the primary force in the new global geopolitical and economic future. Money and power are the motivators, but if staying on top means war, then so be it. Obama's "army of teachers" will be part of the equation that makes sure our military is ever-present, technologically superior, and in a position to protect American corporate dominance. *A Nation at Risk*, the doomsday warning from the 1980s, is still at play and is still advising education policy.

The United States is not number one in international test scores, and that is being used as a cheap way to scare us into believing we are going to sink on the world stage. We need to scan the landscape again and focus on the "power people" who are truly dangerous for our futures. And they all tend to live in large American cities, not foreign lands. They all tend to worry that China and other rising powers are spreading their financial and corporate interests to new parts of the world, creating new infrastructures in formerly undeveloped regions, and posting their flags. In other words, as George Carlin would say, they're cutting in on our action.

As a final thought for this chapter: I'm sure that the schools that the Gates, Obama, Duncan, and other billionaire children go to are much more attuned to providing actual science instruction, as opposed to the standardized workforce training the rest of our kids will receive. Those will be the kids who grow up and are placed in positions to make real changes and innovations. The rest of our kids will be expected to use their high achievements and buildup of knowledge and skills to serve whatever purpose they are needed for.

And, no, we're not going to Mars anytime soon.

CHAPTER

2

The Enemies of Public Education

"Education is wonderfully messy, and (thankfully) usually not efficient in the corporate sense."

– Jennifer Holberg Flood

President Obama's inauguration speech in 2009 mentioned schools exactly twice. The first time to say that they were failing too many kids and the second time to say that they needed to be transformed in order to meet the demands of a new age. He didn't use the words "education," or "teachers," or "students" at all. He used "children" three times, and they were all passive references. All we were told, in this era of economic collapse and war, was that our schools were failing too many of our kids and must be fixed.[28]

In 2009, education wasn't real big on anyone's mind, since this was the anxiety-ridden time when upside-down homes were being taken due to bad (mostly illegal) mortgages, medical coverage was a big talking point, and the country was bleeding jobs out faster than anyone could have predicted. But those two little mentions of our schools meant very big things that were to come, and had actually already been in the works long before Obama took the stage.

Little by little, we started seeing more and more about the newly released results from international tests in math, science, and reading, which were administered in 2009. The message coming in was bleak: The United States was falling behind! We were going to be laughed at! We're doomed!

During the next election cycle, there was more focus on education, with President Obama and Governor Mitt Romney debating more or less about who liked teachers the most. The problem being, of course, that both of these seemingly polar opposites had the exact same plan for education, they just used different strategies to get there. Either way, the base idea was to sell the myth to the American public that schools are a dismal failure and that Corporate America needs to take the reins if we are to survive in the future global economy. Obama's 2013 inauguration speech mentioned teachers and students even less, but drove home the point that our country needs to "reform" its schools and make people learn more and work harder. First, they needed to get teachers out of the bog of the profession in which they are stuck, and then they need to create a curriculum that will really get those kids movin' in the right direction!

It's relatively common knowledge now that the Common Core State Standards Initiative was the work of a non-profit, Achieve, Inc., which includes two trade organizations: the National Governors Association (NGA) and the Council of Chief State School Officers (CCSSO). Achieve, Inc. is a corporate entity made up of financial businesspeople, academics, lobbyists, former lawmakers, and select state governors. They take great pride in being the biggest educational reform company that continues to employ more business leaders, state governors, and policy advisors than actual educators.

Not even a single, currently practicing, K-12 teacher (the few educators on staff were former teachers) took part in the development of these standards. The people creating and working on implementing the Common Core have had very short times in classrooms (if any at all) and many are notable for their degrees in law and public policy.

The campaign in support of the Common Core has been well-orchestrated, increasingly loud, and encompassing of several different venues. While, for the most part, Common Core has remained a silent subject for the public, we are starting to see more and more companies and ad agencies putting out the word on how great it is. We've seen education publishers jump on board to sell their wares, respected authorities on educational technology and institutional development have joined the club, and state governments continue to echo the mantras that Achieve, Inc. coined.

This conversation didn't start with the Obama Administration; it started even before No Child Left Behind, under the George W. Bush Administration. In *Children of the Core*, I spend considerable time with the history of the corporate and government strategies and why this education crisis was created. I won't spend time on that here (that book is still available online), because I want to talk about the players behind this current, and more successful, incarnation of the campaign to sell public schools and narrow our kids' choices for the future.

There are so many different strands in the web of support for the Common Core, it's difficult to make strong or meaningful connections. Some try, but tend to focus too strongly on the agendas or connections that affect them personally or fit their ideologies most closely. Some focus on one set of connections so intently that they end up ignoring others, which leaves out vital information and trends.

In this chapter, I would like to start to decompose the make-up of the web of Common Core and privatization supporters and look at them more closely. There are plenty of agendas and goals at play, but I do believe there are two main objectives. First, let's look at the major players, followed by the smaller pawns involved in adopting and securing the Common Core State Standards. Although I maintain that this is a partnership between government bureaucrats and corporate masters, there is a hierarchy among the money, the power, and the lackeys. And, please, forgive me for not including absolutely everyone. That would be a book all on its own.

The point here is to begin the build a picture of the movement, along with their missions, their connections, and their motives.

Tier One: Big Money

Bill Gates

Let's start at the top. I call this the top because you can find the Bill and Melinda Gates Foundation as a contributor to almost everyone and everything involving education reform. The founder and former CEO of Microsoft, Inc., has been at the center of education reform in the United States since at least as early as the late 2000s. The Bill and Melinda Gates Foundation has pushed around $150 million into the planning, creation, implementation, training, and testing of the standards (plus millions more to organizations that push them forward), and is very publicly vocal about his support as well. It's been consistently reported that this is a philanthropic gesture to level the education playing field, close the racial "achievement gap," provide the necessary preparations for all kids to be ready for the college programs and careers of the 21st century.[29]

Not only that, Bill Gates has been vocal about the effects of teacher preparation on students, suggesting that the single most important factor in a child's education is the teacher in front of the classroom. Building from that notion, the Foundation has created an official Measures of Effective Teaching (MET) system, which is being used as a model in several states around the country. The MET is a system by which data can be systematically collected-- including student test scores, scores from rubrics and frameworks, and other factors--to determine if a teacher is effective or not. The system has been given nods of support from many state education departments, the two national teachers' unions, and the Federal Department of Education.[30]

Speaking of the national teachers' unions: they also receiving a good payment from the Gates Foundation to help fund "professional development," which means training teachers how to use the Common Core, aligned curricula, and prepare for aligned assessments.

Recently, the Gates Foundation has also caused a stir with teachers and parents with such investments as formal classroom videotaping programs and child monitoring technologies. In a TED Talk not too long ago, Bill Gates suggested that 98% of teachers have never gotten "systematic feedback" about their performance. The plan? Videotape them, let a group of peers analyze the tape, and provide "feedback," which may or may not become part of the overall MET.

One of the locations of the videotaping pilot program is the Charlotte Mecklenburg Schools district, where I taught from 2011 – 2012. I was asked to volunteer to participate in the pilot and have my lessons videotaped for my own "development" purposes. I was told that my videos would be kept secure and only released for training purposes with my permission. I do remember sitting in a few meetings where we watched teacher videos and discussed their practices, but we never watched mine. I can neither confirm nor deny the use or security of my own video, since I never heard about them again. I do, however, know that my videos were uploaded to a central database among many others.

Just to throw it right out there: Bill Gates is completely incorrect about the 98%. One of the major pushes for teacher development prior to 2009 was the inclusion of peer and administrative feedback, meaningful discussions about practice, and the ability of professionals to learn from each other. We didn't need a billionaire to invest in something that was happening without him, especially when it's pretty suspect that his intentions are not pure in terms of development.

Two institutional experts, Robert and Rebecca DuFour, created an entire program around the idea and were quite successful touring around the country and helping educators learn how to work together effectively. It was the idea that a professional learning community (PLC) could work closely together to set goals, create actions and evaluations, and use the feedback to continuously improve. I remember attending their conference in 2010, in Salem, Oregon. I remember the message of collegiality and professional interactions. I also attended a seminar in 2012, where the message had changed. What was once all about teachers growing and learning together had become teachers aligning their teaching to common standards, creating and using data from common assessments, and using test scores to attempt to show continuous improvement in preparation for their test-based evaluations. From personal and professional growth to corporate data trends. It's pretty depressing.

The point in talking about the DuFours is that Bill Gates is not the first to suggest a feedback model for teachers. Teachers have been doing that for a very long time without the help of billionaire "philanthropists." We have found that qualitative peer and administrative feedback is much more helpful and meaningful than quantitative data analysis.

Anyway, the idea here is that Bill Gates and his Foundation have taken a very strong public stance that they, with the help of their friends, have figured out how to fix education and get America back to being "globally competitive." They have amassed a very large consortium of supporters (many members of which also don't have any educational experience or expertise) and have been very good at ignoring opposition. I guess when you have enough money to buy the American education system, you also have enough money to plug your ears when those who disagree are talking. There are serious flaws in the Gates ideals of reform, and this book will be spending considerable time looking at those flaws.

Gates stills serves as the chairman of the board for Microsoft, which is the largest software corporation in the world (followed distantly by Oracle and IBM, which are also supporters of Common Core for the reasons I will spell out next). Software and tech corporations—especially big ones—need lots of talented software engineers and coders on staff in order to create new software, fix bugs, monitor performance, and other tasks. Bill

Gates is one of many corporate leaders that suggest, along with the Department of Education, that American higher education does not produce enough highly-qualified science, technology, engineering, and math (STEM) graduates. In fact, in its quest for talent, Microsoft leads the nation in H1-B visa applications to recruit, hire, and employ foreign workers. Why? Because, apparently, there is a shortage of coders in this country and corporations must seek outside of our borders for that talent.

According to recent statistics, about half of college graduates trained in STEM courses of study are currently not working in STEM-related fields. That includes software engineers and coders.[31] This begs the question: why aren't they working at Microsoft? How can there be a shortage of coders if Microsoft is recruiting outside of the U.S.? The quick go-to answer is that Americans aren't qualified, and we need innovative people to drive the economy.

A quick assessment of how American coding graduates feel about all of this brings up frustration, questions, and the search for alternatives--many of them considering leaving America to work for offshored company locations. American coders, who are educated and employed here, look forward to start hourly rates as high as $100 per hour. The frustrated ones (the unemployed ones) report being passed over by foreign talent that will work for as low as one-sixth that rate.

Half of American STEM graduates not employed in STEM fields, large corporations applying for record numbers of H1-B visas to recruit foreign talent, and Americans reporting that their jobs are being given to foreign talent that will work for less. Are we starting to see a connection?

Earlier in 2013, Bill Gates and Mark Zuckerberg (of Facebook notoriety), joined with voices as varied as Ashton Kutcher, will.i.am., and Michael Bloomberg to suggest that every American student should graduate from high school knowing how to code software. They put forward the message that coding is cool, gets you a great job, and anyone can do it. I used to say the same thing about geology. I love Earth science and I believe that anyone who likes to be outside and figure out puzzles, and learn about the world can do it! It's pretty easy really. Geology is based on forces and common sense. And rocks are rocks. It's not like traveling to a new region of the planet and having to learn all new plants, like a botanist would. Rocks are of the general classifications no matter where you go. If you like to travel, dig in the dirt, and write scientific papers on your research, geology is the field for you!

But that was the problem: not everyone likes to do those things. Some people like to other things. Not every kid wants to code. Some people really want to work (for 12 hours a day) in a cool building with other computer people where you can get wholesome lunches and dry cleaning for free. Some people really want to work in front of a computer screen solving problems and creating lines and lines of code. But not everyone does.

The other support behind the idea lies in the suggestion that coding is about thinking. If a kid learns how to code, she is also learning how to think, solve problems, and put pieces together in a logical way. The same argument was used to require that every high school student masters algebra. It's the same argument that I used about geology. It's about thinking. But, you know, lots of different things help students develop students into effective and productive thinkers. Art and music can do it. Writing a musical score requires just as much math and deep and creative thinking (if not more) than software development. Another thing that creates the ability for kids to develop logical and creative thinking? Play.

That's not what this is about, however. The commercial that was produced by Code.org was a piece that tried to sell the idea that this is what kids want. It spent very little time on the idea that it will make America competitive in the global economy, and that's good, because it would be false. The fact is, growing a nation of coders won't do anything for the country as a whole. As I mentioned earlier, there are plenty of coders in the United States already. Somewhere around 4.5% of them are unemployed, with even more software engineers and coders moving on to jobs in fields other than software coding—sometimes you have to take what you can get, and there are not enough jobs for these young grads.

I have been critical of the Common Core for many reasons, which I will describe as we move forward in this book. One of the reasons is because these CEOs want us to believe that we need Common Core to prepare students for a future that is unpredictable using standards that are static. A Kindergarten student who enters the Common Core staircase now will likely receive an education that is obsolete by the time he or she graduates from high school. Bill Gates and other technocrats think they have solved this problem with software. By following the Common Core, these Kindergarteners will be ready to work in the technologically advanced and advancing world. But, not even Bill Gates can predict that.

That doesn't mean he won't try. In a 2009 message to state leadership, Bill Gates stated his excitement about common national standards. He has stated that the alignment of the standards, achievement tests, and data collection systems are the key to school reform—and those who oppose his idea are obviously against real reform. Bill Gates sees reform as the ability to measure teacher performance based on student achievement against the Common Core. He is not shy about selling profit-bearing materials to student for studying for the tests and for remedial purposes. In other words, when kids fail those tests, for-profit corporations should be waiting in the wings to save them with new test prep materials.[32] There is a conflict of interest here, and we will spend some time with that later.

The real problem here, though, comes from the discussion above, regarding STEM graduates. Bill Gates and his friends have very loudly and publicly sold us a fabricated crisis: If American students aren't trained in STEM—with emphasis on computer training—our country will fall behind the rest of the world and sink economically. But, there is absolutely no evidence that this is happening, will happen, or that Race to the Top initiatives could save us even if it were to happen. Bill Gates is interested in one thing and one thing only: saving the corporate giants that hire computer labor. It is the dogma of such companies that they are the guardians of future and to safeguard America's future, they must dominate the world markets. To be sure, according to several tech CEOs, there would be no world market if it weren't for them.

And there may be some truth to that. But, there is currently no crisis in any of this. There is no shortage of qualified STEM graduates, including software engineers. There are plenty of them, and many are very well-qualified as well as highly creative and innovative. Many of them are entrepreneurial—since they can't get jobs with tech giants anyway—and create their own products that do very well on the world market. And that's good! That's the way America should be working: entrepreneurs competing with other entrepreneurs in a fair system which supports that type of work. That would be capitalism. But, that doesn't match Bill Gates' interests. Bill Gates isn't a capitalist.

Bill Gates and friends are pushing for every American high school student to learn coding because it will flood the job market with coders and other computer personnel. This is basic economics. If Microsoft and Oracle and others are recruiting foreign talent because it's cheaper, Bill Gates figures he can be the good guy by telling high school students to prepare themselves for careers by learning to code. That way, he will have a pool of coders (which is already big) so large that it will drive down the wage index for that field—as well as many other fields in computer technology and engineering.

So, there are two separate profit-boosting schemes. One short-term (building a consumer foundation of technology-based educational products and services, especially for response to intervention for failing students) and one long-term (building a skilled workforce big enough to drive down costs, while also preventing too much innovative competition from rising from that pool). It sounds crazy; it sounds like conspiracy theory, but Gates isn't shy about sharing these grand plans. You just have to take the time to read his stuff. (Hint: follow the end notes.)

The bottom line: Bill Gates isn't going to fix education for the benefit of kids or teachers or the United States. Bill Gates is going to "fix" education to produce the cheap, skilled workforce needed for tech giants to remain globally competitive and insanely rich.

Who else is on board the Common Core train, which has apparently "left the station?"

ExxonMobil

Why does ExxonMobil invest so much advertising and lobbying money to get states to adopt the Common Core? They're an oil company. Sure, they need smart people to manage finances, engineer oil and gas extraction techniques and machines, maintain and build refineries, have a solid understanding of geology and mining, and do many other technical and science-related gas and oil things. You would think that ExxonMobil would want free-thinking, creative, and innovative learners coming to their ranks from high school and college. After all, smart oil companies understand that they will need to start adding investments and people to their alternative energy plans in order to stay competitive. The last thing you'd think ExxonMobil would need are common learning standards for the next generation of problem solvers.

Common Core is not the definition of an innovative program. It is strictly a one-size-fits-all set of national standards that leads every K-12 student to a predetermined and corporate-designed end. This one was even hard for Glenn Beck to wrap his mind around in April of 2013. So, why, really does ExxonMobil support the Common Core so strongly?

It's for the exact same reasons—but in a different field—that Bill Gates and Mark Zuckerberg want every high school graduate to know how to code software. Glenn Beck surmised that ExxonMobil wants (or uses) child labor. He almost figured it out, but not quite. ExxonMobil doesn't want kids working for them, yet; they want lots of students trained in the STEM fields related to energy corporate giants so they can have *cheap* labor. The company needs lots and lots of engineers, mechanics, geologists, chemists, engineers and other skilled workers. Those jobs are relatively high-paying jobs, and while Exxon doesn't have nearly as many H1-B visa applications as Microsoft or the other software giants, they do bring in a fair amount of foreign labor to work for a fraction of the cost as American engineers or geologists.[33]

ExxonMobil's website features a very attractive and comprehensive portion for math and science education initiatives and reform ideas, funded by the ExxonMobil Foundation. The overall message here is the same as everywhere else: the United

States is failing and it's because we aren't training our teachers to teach math and science effectively. The Foundation follows the Bill Gates ideal that the best way to fix education is to fix teachers. The best way to fix teachers is to train them to teach the material that benefits the corporate sponsor.

I've actually attended a "development workshop," sponsored by ConocoPhillips (another energy giant), where many other science teachers gathered to receive free materials, free gifts, free lunch, and free professional development--all in the name of teaching a few units on geology, plate tectonics, mining, energy production, and the benefits of "clean" fossil fuels. Did I mention we all got lots of *free* stuff? I got an answer right during an end-of-unit quiz and won a hat. It had the ConocoPhillips logo on it and was actually pretty nice, other than that. I also left with science kits to use in my classroom when I was teaching one of the dozens of lesson plans that I received in a very large ConocoPhillips binder. The kits really were very cool and I did use some of them to teach hands-on lessons. I tended to leave the pre-made lesson plans in the binder, though, since I already know how to teach science to 8th graders. I didn't really think it was necessary to rely on an oil company to help me teach student-centered lessons that require critical thought.

Perhaps that's a problem for corporations like ConocoPhillips and ExxonMobil. Perhaps teachers like me are a problem for them. I didn't do what they expected me to do when I returned to the classroom. These companies obviously spent plenty of money to invest in the idea that they were guiding the science curriculum in areas that affected their plans (the science kit alone was valued at over $500). After all, they are looking to the schools to build their workforce. If the schools are brazen enough to start trying to build corporate or entrepreneurial competitors, or some smart kids that will beat them to the alternative energy race, we're going to have a problem. Correction: *they* will have a problem. We'll actually probably benefit greatly from capitalism working the way it's supposed to.

That's one of the fundamental problems our country faces right now: capitalism doesn't work the way it's supposed to work on paper--but that's a topic for another time.

The point here is that energy giants like ExxonMobil and ConocoPhillips are attempting to join the movement to use public schools to meet their current and future agendas. The main idea is secure global competitiveness (again, for the company, not the kids or the country) and training teachers to train kids is the best strategy they have. More and more people who realize what Common Core is point to government indoctrination as the most dangerous result. I would like us to start worrying more about *corporate* "indoctrination," where our kids are being taught in schools where the curriculum mostly aligns to the standards set by these types of corporations.

I even remember my ConocoPhillips trainer relaying the message that her corporate masters wanted her to tell: alternative energy is a thing of the distant future; we're not there yet. I taught 7th graders at the time, in 2008. Those kids graduated this year, 2013. If ConocoPhillips had their way, my former students would be enrolling in geology and engineering courses. They'll be using what I taught them about plate tectonics and the surface of the Earth to base their careers in the booming industry of hydraulic fracturing, or "fracking," for the extraction of subterranean natural gas. ConocoPhillips is also hoping that enough of them will join the field that the corporations can bring down their salaries.

Recently, the CEO of ExxonMobil, R.W. Tillerson, sent a letter to the office of Pennsylvania Governor Tom Corbett to convey the oil giant's dissatisfaction with Corbett's choice to put the Common Core State Standards on hold, pending further study and consideration.[34] The letter suggests that the Common Core will prepare Pennsylvania kids with the necessary skills for today's workforce, and that the Governor needs to hurry up with his soul-searching and get back to business. Tillerson then reminded Corbett of the money that ExxonMobil has already spent in Pennsylvania, and left with the air that the money and the jobs might not be in Pennsylvania for long if Corbett doesn't pick up the pace and get back to the plan.

The government takes a lot of heat from the groups who worry about dumbing down the curriculum, taking away parents' freedoms, and ruining our kids' ability to think, at the same time that the corporations involved sneak their bribes and threats into states, districts, and schools. As you can see, even if a government entity (like a state governor) does have a moment of clarity, the corporations pulling his strings are quick to correct his out-of-line behavior.

So, we have tech giants and energy giants shilling for the implementation of these standards. Who's next?

The Walton Foundation

The heirs of the Sam Walton fortune are billionaires of the not-so-self-made type, who set up the Walton Family Foundation (WFF)—the philanthropic arm of the Walmart Empire. The Walton Foundation has three missions, one of which is to fix the schooling system in America. Although there is no specific idea from the Foundation's website regarding the actual problems other than "failing" schools, there is plenty to read about what they think will "fix" it.[35] Walton is not hiding anything. They are of the ideological camp that the public schools must be taken out of the equation and that "free-market" strategies should govern the leftovers. The Walton Foundation has given millions in grants to charter "startups" (the word startup is a misnomer, since the charters that have opened under these grants are mostly run under KIPP or other, already-established charter companies) and to politicians that support "parent trigger" laws, closing public schools, and replacing them with charter schools that employ temporary teachers from Teach for America and The New Teacher Project. It has also invested several million dollars to Michelle Rhee's organization, StudentsFirst, to help boost the corporate charter movement.[36]

The Walton Foundation calls its education grants "investments," and never mentions creating learning environments that are designed with kids in mind. To call this a philanthropy is like calling United Healthcare Systems a charity. There is no charity here; this is a business investment, and, just like the Gates and the oil companies, there are both short-term and long-term plans in place to cash in big.

Again, the master plan is the same. Get rid of good teachers who have a bad habit of teaching whole children to live happily and successfully and replace them with unskilled test-preparation associates that can prepare kids to take Common Core tests. If kids can show proficiency on those tests, then they are deemed ready for the workforce I have described. If they are taught to think for themselves, create new ideas and inventions, and show themselves to be just a little too innovative, then they become a threat to the status quo. Walmart doesn't want competitors, either, and it certainly doesn't want a workforce that questions ethics or logic of business practices or even thinks of unionizing.

Walmart hopes to achieve its goals through three initiatives: (1) shaping public policy, which means getting laws passed that allow for more charter schools, fewer or no unions, loss of pensions and tenure, and relaxed requirements for teacher certifications for new charter systems; (2) creating quality schools, which means opening charter schools that can pass CCSS-aligned, standardized tests with higher scores than the public schools can; and (3) improving existing schools, which is a euphemism for getting rid of veteran teachers and administrators and restructuring those schools using new names, new sponsorships, new personnel and new curricula.

The Waltons are not timid about releasing to the public its intentions. They want to effectively destroy the public education system, since the current system does confirm to the plans and goals of large corporations. The Waltons sell it as a failure of schools, but there is no evidence to support that claim. The Foundation is very active in select large cities around the country, many of which we've heard about through education news lately.

Chicago is the site of several clashes between the Chicago Public Schools and the Chicago Teachers' Union. Mayor Rahm ordered the closing of 50 public schools in mostly low-income, racial minority neighborhoods, and CPS recently laid off 850 teachers. The Walton Foundation names Chicago as one of its most important "investment sites," along with Los Angeles; Washington, D.C.; Albany, New York; New Orleans; and Phoenix-- all cities where more and more schools are being closed, budgets are being slashed, and teachers are being let go.

The Walton Foundation believes that in order to fix the education system, which we know isn't broken, you have to completely ruin the system in place and replace it with a new, narrower focus.

The Foundation suggests that this is all in the name of "school choice." If the actions taking place in these investment sites is of any indication, the choice has become forced. In other words, there is no choice. Once a school is closed in a poor neighborhood, the students of the school are selected to attend other schools or the charter school that has opened in its place. Often, these children don't have the transportation to get to a new school, and education budgets being passed in those cities don't include increases to accommodate the greater need.

The Gates Foundation needs a new customer base for electronic teaching and remediation materials, as well as a cheap workforce for the future. Oil companies want a larger pool of dedicated workers for their operations, as well. What does a retail giant hope to gain from the future of rigidly trained and compliant students in publicly-funded, privately-held charters? Or is that even part of their investment plan?

While some of the earlier Walton statements were about trying to ensure quality education for all children, more recent public statements have been to the tune of Walmart's difficulties in finding qualified personnel for entry-level workers at Walmart. So, although that seems ridiculous, it does resonate with the statements of the tech and oil folks. There is also the hard-to-ignore fact that Walton pushes its influence into low-income and mostly Black and Hispanic neighborhoods in economically-depressed urban centers, like the investment sites mentioned earlier.

In her bestselling book, *The Death and Life of the Great American School System*, Diane Ravitch warns of the undemocratic relinquishment of community and parental power to large corporate foundations, where there is no way to back out.[37] You cannot vote out corporate power, especially when it's contracted in poor, underrepresented communities like the ones that Walton targets. The Foundation has deep connections with policymakers and lobbyists that push for privatization and voucher systems, which demand strict (and increasingly unfair) accountability measures for public schools and teachers, but demand no such measures for the charter organizations they support.

The bottom line for the Walton Foundation seems to be much less about schools, kids, and communities than it is about investing in a system that will not only get them a cash ROI, but also the spread of a privatization ideology that has gotten them where they are now. Walmart is a fiercely anti-union corporation, which is well-known for business practices that keep employment costs down at the expense of workers. Walmart grows under the assumptions that low-wage, unstable jobs, and few benefits leads to a world where competition boosts the profits of companies like theirs. That's the world they wish to build at the expense of our kids and the future of America. A company as shady as this should not be allowed near our schools, much less running them.

The Broad Foundation

Eli Broad is a real estate billionaire who has decided to save the world. Same as the Waltons, he believes that getting rid of public schools and replacing them with charters, staffed by barely-trained and temporary teachers from Teach for America, will save America. Eli takes a much more hardline stance in this game, though: he blames education for just about all of society's ills, from college dropout rates, to unemployment, to crime, to being noncompetitive in the global economy.[38] The Eli and Edythe

Broad Foundation operates with much the same goals as the Walton Foundation, but with probably a bit more crass.

Like the Waltons, the Broad Foundation lists as its first initiative the shaping of public policy. Eli is a major campaign contributor to the Democratic Party and the current administration under Obama. Broadly speaking (pardon the pun), the Foundation seeks to affect education reform in two major ways: "programs," which are focused on a certain geographic locations and populations, or "pipelines," which generate trained personnel to be placed in high-level positions that are able to then affect Broad-desired changes. (The pipeline scenario also bypasses the need for affecting public policy, since the change begins to happen from *within* a targeted system.)

Also like the Waltons, the Broads funnel their money and their efforts into driving local public education in the direction they see fit. The Broad Foundation is a little different in that it invests into its training programs for superintendents and leadership, as described above. Using alternative certification programs and placing their "products" into suffering districts, change can be made from within, and the accountability for the change is held to teachers and schools.

Parents Across America, a public school advocacy group, has a comprehensive white paper about the workings, consequences, and personnel of the Broad programs.[39] In it, they point out the following:

> In addition, the foundation offers free diagnostic "audits" to school districts, along with recommendations

aligned with its policy preferences. It produces a number of guides and toolkits for school districts, including a "School Closure Guide," based on the experiences of Broad-trained administrators involved in closing schools in Boston, Charleston, Chicago, Dallas, Washington, D.C., Miami-Dade County, Oakland, Pittsburgh, St. Louis, and Seattle.

In other words, the Broad Foundation holds experience and expertise in "turning around" or closing schools, which means getting them to fail first, using *free* diagnostic audits. Once the plans materialize, and failure begins to show up, other Broad-funded groups show up to save the day (e.g., StudentsFirst and Parent Revolution). The Foundation also makes large contributions to political candidates that promise to move legislation favorable to closing schools, opening more charters, firing teachers, and allowing states to offer alternative certification programs to new teachers. They even offer a handy guide in their "toolkit" for closing schools quickly and efficiently, including how to deal with community opposition, scattering dislocated students, and dealing with disenfranchised students, families, and staff.[40]

The three big foundations—the Gates, the Waltons, and the Broads—have one more incredibly powerful and dangerous thing in common and in cooperation: they offer contributors and contributions to major media outlets to press their message into the public sphere, mostly unopposed, and with plenty of vocal support from the networks. National Public Radio (NPR) receives grant money from all three to the tune of over $3 million. Other networks (even for-profit networks) have also reportedly seen generous gifts from the big three.[41]

In 2007, the Gates and Broad Foundations ponied up $60 million to the National Governors Association (NGA) and the Council of Chief State School Officers (CCSSO) in support of developing common standards in K-12.

All three have levied funding toward other organizations—local, state, and national—in order to create buy-in and support for the initiatives under Race to the Top, Common Core, and school reform. These three Foundations have proven their power through money, and their dangerous intentions by the acts that have occurred thanks to their financing.

ALEC

Among many other things, the American Legislative Exchange Council (ALEC) has been working hard to create model legislation to push the states to change or add laws allowing more and more corporate charter organizations into the mix. As we continue to see the artificial failures of teachers and schools—and, consequently, the closing of those public schools—we are also seeing more legislation that allow increasing numbers of charter schools to take over those schools, and allow public dollars to fund those schools.

The members of ALEC in the education domain receive funding and support from a list of non-educators and "reformy" corporations, such as ExxonMobil and State Farm. They also enjoy support from a list of state representatives and senators (almost all Republican). Their primary function in all of this is to talk secretly about how to carve up America's public school system among the elite and how to use public education funding into big profits for large investors.

The education model projects that have become the focus of ALEC's work support and advance the whims and fancies of the "big three" above. Most aggressive are the causes of "choice" (charter takeovers), vouchers, and parent trigger legislation.[42]

I won't spend too much time with this organization, since they leave everything open to the public, except their meetings. Browse the website http://www.alec.org sometime, and spend some time with their list of government representatives and private members. I will speak a little more about some of these members at the end of the book.

National Council on Teacher Quality (NCTQ)

In June of 2013, The NCTQ released its assessment report on the quality of university-level teacher preparation programs. To quickly summarize, the best schools were still not optimal, and most programs simply failed the test of NCTQ's scrutiny. In other words, America's teachers are not qualified to teach in their first year out of college due to the lack of preparation they get from their trainings.[43]

Who is NCTQ and why did they flunk America's teaching programs?

NCTQ is an organization advised by Pearson's Chief Education Advisor, Sir Michael Barber, who is joined by an array of charter school cheerleaders, founders, and other privatization network personnel. Leading the charge is Barbara O'Brien, president of Get Smart Schools, which is another Teach for America (TFA) and Walton-funded organization dedicated to training school leaders, much as the Broad Foundation does, and is currently gutting Denver schools to make room for corporate takeover. Funding this organization is a list of the usual suspects in corporate reform: Gates, Broad, Walton, Dell, Carnegie, Anschutz, and so on, and so on.

NCTQ describes itself as a multi-partisan group that advocates for changes in the ways that teachers are recruited, trained, retained, and compensated. The fact is, this is nothing more than a large, well-funded think tank, which uses its own criteria (made in alignment with the ideologies of the funding organizations) to rate and rank schools, districts, and states based on teaching policies. They have also been accused of using highly questionable research tactics and methods, and for targeting schools and districts that do not follow the methods and models of the established corporate teacher training and charter organizations (e.g. KIPP and TFA).

There are two serious problems with this organization's practices, regardless of the methodology of their studies:

1. They are seeking means to an end. Yes, that's bad science, and it negates their research results. But, they are not trying to do science; they are trying to justify the

takeover of public university programs and replace them with privately-run programs using public dollars. This study is an investment analysis, not a scientific analysis. They already know the goal. They will work tirelessly to seek (or make up) data that proves that their plans to privatize university teacher-training programs are relevant and necessary.

2. There were no longitudinal data involved at all, and only about 1% of the nation's teacher prep programs were included in the study, which were selected not-so-much at random. No one followed the success of randomly selected teachers from the programs into the classrooms and further. Most of the data was collected from first year teachers who said they didn't feel prepared. Here's a question: how many first-year teachers have ever felt totally prepared? Teaching is a growth practice—we learn and we get better as we go.

I was given a mentor during my first year, which was incredibly helpful. Many school districts engage in the mentor practice, since it gives new teachers someone to reflect with and learn and get feedback from. The study from the NCTQ said that most universities do not have proper intern or residency programs or selection criteria that are *rigorous* enough (there's that word again). On the contrary, almost all university programs require a student-teaching semester or year. And "selection criteria" sounds suspect, since teachers go into teaching for many reasons, but soon find out if they are qualified or not. A selection criteria for all teacher candidates would thin the candidate pool to only the teachers who can pass tests or other "predict the future" scenarios, no doubt developed by Pearson. Indeed this is already happening. Read about edTPA evaluations, which is part of the plan above, and universities are being pressured to participate, at risk of losing accreditation.[44]

Teacher candidates develop as they go. I feel I'm a testament to that as well. NCTQ seeks to do to teacher-prep students what its friends are doing to K-12 students: quantize them and push them through a system that puts them into a classroom ready to teach students how to prepare for and pass tests.

The National Center for Teacher Quality is a bogus organization, since it comes to us from a non-scientific point of view and tons of people who know next to nothing about teaching. When an agenda and a bunch of policy ideas are predetermined, and the studies comes later, you know something's going on. But the media sure grabbed on to the latest study it like it was some sort of super-breakthrough, newsworthy piece of action! Even NPR did some spots on their radio network about this study, which were less than balanced. I'm talking, of course, about the Teacher Prep Review.

And, of course, the report itself was never expected to be a scientific study of any kind, since the list of directors and funders for NCTQ includes the usual suspects of private astroturfers, corporate charter supporters, and foundations that are in line to make money off of investments in the failures of public schools. Looking just a little further shows that other investors are also looking forward to what comes of this, especially those who are in the business of mass producing teachers.

During the campaigns of 2008 and 2012, as President Obama was talking about his "army of teachers," which had specific targets of STEM and early childhood education, ALEC and several others were listening. In 2011, Sen. Michael Bennet, of Colorado, wrote a letter to Obama suggesting that he put it all into motion.[45] Last year, the White House implemented the program to the tune of $100 million in Race to the Top grants. We apparently need 100,000 new teachers. Teach for America only coughs out 4,000 per year.

This year, without coincidence, NCTQ tells us all that teachers are not adequately prepared for the classroom in the first year. How many teachers work in this country? How many will retire? How many will enter the workforce from college? How many are laid off every year? Do these people seriously think we need 100,000 teachers? Well, yeah, if we're to graduate those million new STEM graduates over the next decade. Wait. *One million*? Same questions as the teachers. Half of our STEM graduates can't find STEM jobs, and we need *one million more*?

I'm probably not alone in saying that I was not prepared for my first teaching assignment either. That's because I was nervous and overwhelmed. But, having a mentor and a few years of previous learning, cognition, and teaching theory under my belt smoothed things out pretty quickly.

Universities are now being offered grants from the government and non-profit foundations to start training people who already have bachelor's degrees to become master teachers in STEM. Those master teachers are then expected to go into buildings and start making changes from the inside—specifically, teaching young teachers how to teach common standards and assessments.[46] Sound familiar?

When you're trying to take over public education for the sake of profits and building a future workforce, it's important to cover all of your bases. Let's see:

1. Get legislation passed in order to standardize learning with common standards and assessments.
2. Use the media to demonize teachers, their unions, and tell the world they are failing our kids.
3. Support sweeping Federal mandates to set up kids, teachers, and schools to fail.
4. Make sure your friends at ALEC are writing legislation to help you quickly and efficiently close those schools, fire those teachers, and relocate the students to publicly-funded, privately-run charter schools in which you've invested.
5. Give money to some friends to set up a fake research organization to make teacher prep programs look bad (NCTQ).
6. Take over federally and state-funded university teacher preparation programs with the help of accreditation organizations (who are being blamed also), as well as Race to the Top's money, Pearson's curriculum, and the investments of the Waltons, Gates, and Broads.

7. Profit!

Rupert Murdoch

I am going to talk about the NewsCorp CEO briefly here, because he is a solid player in the private technology and information administration sector of education reform. Murdoch founded the educational division of his huge conglomerate, called *Amplify*, to start finding new ways to cut in on all the action happening in the public school market. Rupert Murdoch certainly has no interest in public schools, freedom of thought, or the ability of our kids to grow up happy, successful, and mindful, so I can only deduce that this venture was purely for investment. Another large piece of evidence for my statement is the fact that Murdoch hired Joel Klein, the New York City butcher of public schools (see Tier 3), to create and launch the K-12 moneymaking machine.

The mission of the company should be enough to make seasoned teachers and authentic historians cringe:

> *Amplify is reimagining the way teachers teach and students learn. We enable teachers to manage whole classrooms and, at the same time, empower them to offer more personalized instruction, so that students become more active, engaged learners.*[47]

So, it's basically another of the dozens of astroturf groups that are trying so hard to make current teachers sound completely inept and worthless (and obsolete). According to Amplify, we need help managing *entire* classrooms and getting to know our kids so that we might engage them. But then Amplify gets a little more honest. What they really want is to support districts (i.e. sell them Amplify technology) as they move forward in their "digital transitions." This goes right along with the Bill Gates philosophy that classes should be much larger and the technology should be doing all the work. It fits into Pearson's vision of the future, where the teacher is just a glorified, yet small-scale systems administrator, constantly monitoring which students have completed which computer module, and then assigning new ones based on "the needs" of those students. Somehow, we've let educrats and reformers determine what our students "need," and they are way off. Finally, it fits very well into the goals and ideologies of everyone discussed in this chapter—replace highly-trained and well-educated teachers with, well, anyone who can use a computer, pretty much. Here's how Murdoch and Klein are making this happen.

In March 2013, at the SXSW conference in Austin, Texas, Klein proudly announced that Amplify will be offering digital curriculum materials *and* its own tablet computer that districts can purchase to run those materials. The tablets are $349 each, roughly the same price as those awful netbooks everyone seemed to love, but districts can save $50 a piece if they subscribe to a two-year contract to receive Amplify's digital curricular materials for $99 per year.[48]

Joel Klein believes that Amplify will be successful because "we understand technology and we understand education." Strange words coming from one of the foremost names in school destruction. However, both the Pearson Learning Corporation and Randi Weingarten, president of the American Federation of Teachers, seem to support the purchase and deployment of these devices, as long they are designed for schoolchildren. Klein suggests that districts can rely on their Race to the Top grant disbursements to purchase and maintain the tablets, without thought to the relatively few states, and even fewer districts, that have actually received money, and for which that money is already running out for implementation of Common Core and testing programs.

On the other hand, some state education departments and districts are looking the other way due to News Corp's recent scandal involving wire-tapping violations and spying on private citizens. Oddly, New York State is one of those that have put the brakes on considering this technology, due to the risk involved in tracking and monitoring students. This is *really* odd since New York State is the only state to choose to sign on to the private inBloom data storage system (of which News Corp. is also a part), which collects and stores student and teacher data and has come under scrutiny for its lack of security protocols, along with Arne Duncan's decision to loosen the restrictions of the FERPA privacy laws.[49]

Amplify is not necessarily a pioneer in this market. Amazon, Barnes & Noble, Microsoft, and Apple have all been marketing their tablet technology for years, with Pearson as the main deliverer of digital curricula. Amplify suggests that it is different, since it can offer hardware, software, and data tracking as a package deal. Many, including me, don't necessarily see that as a good thing. Especially when inBloom is waiting at the end.

Tier Two: The Government

Marc Tucker

Here's a name that most people haven't heard, and I add him here because he is one of the original brains behind the standards-based reform movement, among other things. He's also the link that shows that common national standards, data mining, and Federal and corporate control of the public education system all lead to the national preparation of and training for a workforce. Marc Tucker's vision was put in writing in a lengthy letter to former First Lady Hillary Clinton in 1992, which is now publicly known as the "Dear Hillary" letter.[50] In it, he discusses and markets his vision of a new "human resources development system" for the United States, focusing on education as the engine to power his vision. And his intention was to completely redesigned public education from the inside and outside in order to make his dream a reality.

First, just a little background on Mr. Tucker.

Mr. Tucker has been an education "reformer" since 1989, although he has never taught in a K-12 school. With degrees in several fields (but not education), he has taken on roles such as president of the National Board of Professional Teaching Standards (NBPTS) and several other standards-based lobbying programs. He founded, and is the current president and CEO of the National Center on Education and the Economy (NCEE), which, in 1992 (the same year Agenda 21 was drafted), created the New Standards Project. The project was a collaboration between 23 state and 6 city leaders (also not educators) to create common academic standards and the assessment frameworks to evaluate teachers and students.[51]

In other words, Marc Tucker is the godfather of the Common Core State Standards and the national testing consortia—PARCC and SBAC—we are using today. Additionally, the NCEE launched the National Alliance for Restructuring Education (NARE), in 1989, which was charged with the task of increasing student achievement on standardized tests in urban schools. This means promoting "voucher" systems, corporate charter organizations, and one-size-fits-all curricula. The same year that NARE came about, the NCEE also created the Commission on the Skills of the American Workforce to begin the process of turning learning institutions into workforce training centers. NCEE has worked closely with Pearson Corporation in these endeavors.

NCEE has also worked in the creation of education leadership academies (in much the same way as the Broad Foundation) and final exit exams for high school seniors. Four non-governmental organizations (NGOs) have been qualified to offer those exams so far: ACT, College Board's AP program, the International Baccalaureate program, and the University of Cambridge's International Examinations.

In 1992, very soon after creating the New Standards Project, Tucker wrote a letter to Hillary Clinton (known as the "Dear Hillary" letter) explaining the work and the goals of the NCEE. In it, he laid out plans for restructuring the Federal government into a seamless "human resources development system." In that letter, he markets the attractiveness of common national standards and "a consistent system of unending skill development that begins in the home with the very young and continues through school, postsecondary education and the workplace." Here are the precursors to the Common Core State Standards and the P-20 initiative currently championed by the Obama Department of Education.

Tucker did tell Hillary that we would need to "internationally benchmark" our standards, but that they would be especially created for the unique needs of American workers. Also, the assessments, curriculum, pedagogy, and teacher preparation would be tightly aligned to those standards. Other smaller, yet familiar, items include teacher evaluation, merit pay, and free college for three years.

I mention Marc Tucker to illustrate that the programs included in Race to the Top have been on the table for quite some time. Interestingly, it would have been virtually impossible for Bill Clinton to have enacted most of these measures during his administration, as he had a hard enough time keeping standardized testing in place as a measure to determine Title I funding. George W. Bush did not enact Tucker's agenda in full either, using only small pieces that were accepted by his administration and Congress. It took the Chicago Club—Obama, Duncan, and Rahm Emanuel as the leaders—and what Diane Ravitch calls the "billionaire boys' club"—Gates, Walton, Broad— to get education reform to look like Tucker's. Keep in mind that Tucker's NCEE has been very busy ever since 1989, and continues to share its wisdom with many.

President Obama and Arne Duncan

The brain trust behind the competition known as Race to the Top is comprised of two good buddies, which were part of the "Chicago Club," as some have come to call them. It's difficult for Democrats and many teachers to come to terms with the idea that Barack Obama is turning out to be one of the biggest corporate puppets in our history (sorry to say so, but "Obamacare" was basically a fist-bump to the insurance companies and not enough high-five to the American people), especially in the world of education reform. I know that painful dissonance; I used to be a Democrat. Regardless of how many Republicans might say, "I told you so," I believed that this was a man who had a real vision for American to get back on track and to make it a better place to live. I believed that he would turn the destructive policies from the previous eight years, which were hard on the poor, the elderly, the children, and the brave soldiers that have been in harm's way for way too long. I believed.

I'm also not blind. There are red flags surrounding every politician these days, and they are often ignored. (Who has time to look into every one?) It became almost immediately clear to me that, after the 2009 inauguration, we were not going to be getting the president we all thought we were. The American Recovery and Reinvestment Act (ARRA, also known as "the Stimulus") of that year had specific goals, or so we were told: save and create jobs; provide temporary relief for those effected by the recession; and invest in healthcare, education, and infrastructure. Unfortunately, for many reasons, which I will not go into here, it was largely of minimal and temporary effect.

The ARRA investment in education included $80 billion for K-12 education, with most of that many set to offset state shortfalls and prevent layoffs and program cuts. Of the roughly $5 billion leftover, the Obama Administration started a contest to see which states were going to jumped into the "reform" movement first. The previous chapter talks more about that.

What I often hear from Obama supporters is that Arne Duncan is the mastermind behind the reform agenda behind Race to the Top and the national standards, testing, and data requirements. I wish could I could agree that Obama doesn't really understand the implications, but I don't. I believe that Arne has certainly put in his own ideas and programs, but other than that, he is simply following his boss's order. This has been the plan from the beginning, and Obama is very much in charge. Arne

Duncan, however, is the most vocal, so I will focus on some of what he has said about his—and Obama's—vision for American education.

In November of 2010, Duncan addressed the United Nations Educational, Scientific, and Cultural Organization (UNESCO) in Paris, France.[52]   The speech makes it known that this Administration has chosen to recognize a constructed crisis and has come up with a very large, all-encompassing plan to overhaul and design the America's education system according to their agenda. He starts by talking of peace, health, and education for all (the rise of America's skilled workforce doesn't have to be part of a zero-sum game), and then continues to suggest that the world's most important need is an economically strong United States. Experts can debate this. I won't.

What is interesting about Duncan's speech is that he leaves out any indication that American is the place of freedom to choose or think for oneself; he leaves out any indication of our country being the place where a child can dream, explore, think, and discover his or her way to a happy and successful life. We used to consider our diversity of choice as a boon to the success of our nation.   Scientists, engineers, computer scientists, musicians, artists, entrepreneurs, explorers, and every other life choice added to the dynamic of our national culture. Arne Duncan and Barack Obama are apparently willing to trade all of that for the chance to be technologically and economically number one in the world.

The plan? Nationalize curriculum, reform accountability for student achievement—which this Administration thinks will reduce the dropout rate—and boost the college graduation rate. First of all, there is no evidence or reason to believe that common standards and curricula, along with testing, will affect dropout or graduation rates. Second of all, the agenda has nothing to do with helping kids. This administration does not care about our children or their futures (nor did the last administration). This is about numbers for dollars, not kids.

Duncan, himself, noted that 2,000 high schools (roughly 10% of the total number) produce over half of the dropouts in the country, yet went on to suggest that sweeping nationwide reforms are the only way to fix that. He called the attempts to help those schools reduce dropout rates, up to this point, "tinkering," and that it isn't working. He did not talk at all about the fact that our dropout rates have been falling steadily over the past two decades, or why he doesn't support further targeted reform to continue fixing the problem. Only national, sweeping reform of all schools can fix this, according to the Obama Administration. What's good for the goose, apparently.

Duncan has also infamously noted that our current educational "crisis" is the civil rights issue of our time. This was close to the same time that he called Hurricane Katrina the best thing that could have happened to New Orleans schools, since it uncovered troubling symptoms of a system gone wrong. I do agree that New Orleans schools had serious problems, especially regarding equitable access in low-income areas. I also understand that this was a community that was already under siege from NCLB-related state reform policies. Duncan called the school system that rose from Katrina's wake "vibrant" and "fast-improving," and took credit for higher graduation rates and scores. Those who were paying attention, however, knew that the incremental gains were being seen before state takeover of the public schools systems. The data from that progress was craftily integrated into the new data from state and charter takeover and sold as proof that Race to the Top programs would work.

The rest of Duncan's speech to UNESCO summarizes the Obama Administration's belief that the Federal role in education should be much more aggressive and involved, and that the rest of the world needs to continue seeing the United States as the leader of everything great, including education. While several opponents of Obama and Common Core have stated that they believe Duncan's cooperation with UNESCO is another step toward the "new world order," I read it more as another step in trying to reclaim and solidify the world's understanding and acceptance of the dominance of American corporations and their leadership into the 21st century. Yes, there is certainly an air of "globalization," here, but it isn't in a utopian sense; this is American government and corporate leadership staking their claims to what they have already decided belongs to them: power, wealth, and the population.

Obama and Duncan are not socialists or communists, by any means. They are neoliberals, which lean much further to the right, pander to corporate power, and have global economic dominance on the brain. In fact, in terms of the ongoing discussions attempting to connect the Common Core Standards to Agenda 21 (and, by extension, Rio +20), I don't believe that Obama is the figure to watch. Using the Kyoto Protocol and other world energy consortia as examples, we can see that the United States has not been too keen on sacrificing economic dominance for the good of the world's needs. Congress never signed off on Agenda 21 and President Obama didn't even attend the Rio +20 conference. Also, as can be expected, the non-governmental organizations (NGOs) from the United States and elsewhere have been highly critical of some things left out of the big plan. I expect that the American NGOs have chosen to go it alone, using their own ideas and their own money to build their own roadmap to "sustainability" goals (and by sustainability, I mean less overhead and more profits).

This discussion is outside of the scope of this book, however, and I will leave it with one more idea: the sustainability processes in American government, while based on the global initiatives, do not appear to be working on a Federal level in cooperation with the United Nations. I will concede that I am not an expert on this, and that I have been seeking the connection between U.S. education reform and Agenda 21 and have not found anything concrete. If anything, it appears that the Unites States, once again, is choosing to break away from the global stage and do their own thing, with the hope and plan of being faster, stronger, and in a position to control the actions of others.

Whether one is better than the other is debatable, but the evidence of America's economic and governmental strategies does not fit a global view or willingness to sacrifice autonomy or sovereignty in the name of a planetary collaboration. However, it is certainly a good idea to start paying attention to what your *individual cities* are doing in terms of the global sustainability movement. While much of it is touted as a program of beneficial projects to rebuild infrastructure and energy technologies, I have already seen cases where public schools (and other institutions, including private property) are sacrificed for those goals.

Rahm Emanuel

Rahm is another member of the Chicago Club (along with Obama and Duncan) and he has made quite an image for himself lately. Emanuel is the current mayor of Chicago, after serving as President Obama's chief of staff (and after a long history of influential positions in politics, where he seemed to leave a trail of alleged scandals and bad blood), and has chosen to continue Arne's Duncan's school reform legacy, back when Arne was CEO of the Chicago Public Schools (CPS). In fact, Emanuel's education policy in Chicago is basically a microcosm of Race to the Top.

One of Emanuel's primary concerns once taking office was pension reform, especially for teachers (it's not too hard to see that as a euphemism for *cutting* and *absorbing* pensions), and cutting other costs in city government. In 2012, the Chicago Teachers Union (CTU) authorized a weeklong strike due to the stalemate in bargaining for healthcare costs, teacher evaluations based on test scores, and other impassables. Emanuel had no intention of bending to their needs or demands and spent most of that time seeking legal assistance to put them back to work.

The Enemies of Public Education

Since the end of the strike, the Emanuel-appointed CEO, Barbara Byrd-Bennett, and her board have ordered closed over 50 schools in mostly poverty-stricken and non-white neighborhoods. Despite the anti-closure protests and resolutions from teachers, students, parents, citizens, and legislators, Byrd-Bennett looked the other way and Emanuel went skiing. It's been pretty well established that the closed schools will be fed to the charter school sharks that are circling in the water, with some buildings being sold to other private businesses on the cheap and with impressive tax breaks.

Just this past July, CPS also made the move to pass out a revolting 1,000 pink slips to teachers (in addition to over 1,000 other school employees) throughout Chicago, citing budget concerns.[53] It was well known that, at the same time, CPS granted $1.6 million to Teach for America, which is an increase of about 325 TFA corps members from the already 270 that are entering their second year. It takes some pretty intense effort to ignore the connections here. Emanuel has also granted money to several other private, non-education systems wishing to set up throughout the city. It seems that he has no faith in the ability of public education to strengthen and cement a community; instead, condominiums and cosmopolitan restaurants and shops are his idea of a better Chicago.

Also, despite pleas and requests from teachers and other constituents across the nation, neither President Obama nor Secretary Duncan made any serious statements or movements regarding the 50 closed schools (they both made general,

98

noncommittal statements regarding the 30+ schools slated for closure in Philadelphia this summer). Perhaps Chicago is one of the small-scale experiments being run by the government and its corporate sponsors. As Chicago goes, so go the rest of our city schools?

Chicago has problems schools, just like every large urban center (and several rural and suburban schools as well). When the mayors of those cities—or, in the case of New York State, the governors and education commissioners—start taking over the school system without allowing the fixes to actually take place and without funding them adequately, we should know that this is not about kids or low-income neighborhoods. This has nothing to do with eradicating poverty, as the reformers continue to say they're doing. This has only to do with burying the poverty or kicking it out of the city as quickly and quietly as possible. Again, moving wealth from the poor to the rich.

Jeb Bush

The former governor of Florida and founder of the Foundation for Excellence in Education (FEE), Jeb Bush, is one of the most active and loudest politicians in the big reform club. The main focus of FEE seems to be changing schools by taking over state education departments. Its mission, vision, and agenda are all very vague and echo the same statements and philosophies as the other big-money organizations and foundations, but FEE's actions speak much louder than words.

Before getting too much into his new foundation, let's look at Jeb's education record as Florida's former governor. Many of the initiatives he began or carried over shed much light on the things he is trying to accomplish now, only nationwide. Just as a quick catch-up, know that this is the second son of George H.W. Bush and the younger brother of George W. Bush. Jeb served as Florida's governor from 1999 to 2007, the whole time that his older brother was in office as the United States president. As governor, Jeb oversaw policies that greatly increased the number and the role of standardized tests in Florida's public schools. His *A+ Plan* put into place a statewide school grading system, based on scores from those tests, which also provided the base of the funding system for schools.[54]

Bush also strongly supported charter takeover of "failing" schools and vouchers for students who attended those schools (again, "failing" is a label solely reflecting test scores). Bush proposed getting rid of state-mandated caps on class size and a refusal to increase taxes for school bonds. Both of those measures did not come to play as legislation, and Bush suffered a reputation as a leader who did not have Florida's children's best interests in mind with his policies. Unfortunately, this seems to be the case even today.

Bush's FEE organization states on its website that the reason it exists is to reverse the "trend" of low American scores on international test scores, since that's the only evidence that FEE uses to support the supposed crisis. Apparently, according to Bush, those low scores mean the end of American economic "dominance." The organization believes that our economy needs "a growing number of educated and skilled workers."[55]

FEE's reform agenda has nothing to do with children, and everything to do with ideology: making money for corporate investors and privatizing public schools. Here are the FEE action items for that agenda:

1. Support the Common Core State Standards being used in all schools, as a rigorous curriculum.

2. Use digital technology to provide individual lesson plans for each student (see Pearson and Rupert Murdoch).

3. Recruit teachers from all professions, regardless of their ability to teach, regardless of their training in the classroom, and regardless of their certification or licensure. Evaluate teachers based on test scores, reward high scoring teachers, fire low scoring teachers, and create merit pay schemes (which have no evidence of efficacy).

4. Make sure all 3rd graders can read on grade level, according to test scores, and enact punitive interventions if they can't (retention, longer school days, loss of recess and play time, etc.).

5. Only fund schools based on outcomes (test scores), as opposed to "seat-time funding." It's my opinion that both outcome *and* seat-time funding are bad policies for schools. It's a shame that this organization is so short-sighted that it can't find alternatives.

6. Promote vouchers, charter growth, and virtual schools in every state, at the expense of public schools.

7. Maintain or increase standardized testing levels in every state, and use those test scores to place grades (A-F) on every school and every state. The data and accountability model for FEE relies on simplicity, regardless of actual utility.

If a lot of those items (or all of them) sound very familiar, it's because they are the same reform items that all of the foundations above are calling for. So, it shouldn't be too surprising that you will find many of the usual suspects in FEE's donors list: Bloomberg, Gates, Walton, Broad, GE, and other notables. FEE, therefore, is just another arm of the "venture philanthropies" that are currently attempting to takeover and redesign public education for corporate and government use.

More specifically, FEE uses its influence to place vetted reformers into state education chief positions around the country, with the cooperation of the state governors. So far, eight chiefs have been placed in states where governors have been lobbied: New Mexico, Maine, Louisiana, New Jersey, Rhode Island, Florida, Oklahoma, and Tennessee. Only Oklahoma's chief is elected by state citizens (the other chiefs are appointed, either by the governor or the state board of education), and she has already been headlined in that state's papers for her destructive and anti-public-school funding policies.

Other newsworthy state chiefs are (I strongly encourage you to Google search their biographies): Tony Bennett (FL), Deborah

Gist (RI), Kevin Huffman (TN), and Chris Cerf (NJ). Relatively unknown is Hanna Skandera (NM), who was appointed by Governor Susana Martinez in 2010, but still has not been confirmed by the State Senate. She is an interesting one to keep an eye on, since she served as Jeb Bush's Secretary of Education, and has tried to implement many of the old Florida policies in New Mexico. There is no doubt that FEE wants badly to spread its influence to other states, and it's very important for citizens to watch their state education policies closely and make it known that this organization and the implants they want to send into education departments are not welcome.

Tier Three: The Action Heroes and the Hired Help

David Coleman

When I go around to speak to different anti-Common Core groups, I notice that there is one name that is not very well known. Everyone seems to know right away who Bill Gates, Michelle Rhee, and other major players are. Many have still not heard of David Coleman, the lead architect of the Common Core State Standards, and the primary author of the English-language arts standards. He graduated with English literature and philosophy degrees, and once applied for a teaching job, but was turned down.

So, the next best step for Coleman was to work for McKinsey & Company, a consultant group for global industries, including urban education. It was a better paying gig, I'm sure, and he took his experience into business for himself to design efficient assessment techniques for schools. Coleman went on his own with the GROW Network, which contracted pretty significantly with Duncan's Chicago Schools to put in place data collection and accountability systems. McGraw-Hill, a private textbook and test publisher acquired Coleman's venture (called the GROW network), and Coleman left McGraw-Hill in 2007. McGraw-Hill still contracts with CPS to this day.

He then helped create the Student Achievement Partners (SAP), which was a lead force in creating the Common Core Standards and is highly focused on outcome-based education (i.e. corporate-model education). He became a major voice for the support of his precious standards, touring the country and selling state leaders and district personnel on their promise and efficacy, neither of which had any evidence behind them. Several of his speeches make his philosophy clear: that the world isn't going to "give a shit what you think," so why should we be teaching our kids to start thinking outside of the box and with creative flair.[56] According to Coleman (a philosophy major, remember), our high school graduates should leave the school system ready to follow company policy, do what they're told, and remain focused on their work alone.[57]

Coleman also served as a founding member of Michelle Rhee's StudentsFirst, which you will read more about later. Knowing that he's aligned with Michelle Rhee's anti-teacher and anti-public school ideology should be enough to discredit him. He was picked up in the Fall of 2012 as the CEO of College Board, which creates, administers, and sells the SAT test, the AP

program, and several other education evaluation materials. Coleman has stated that the SAT test and the AP program will soon be aligned to the Common Core State Standards, effectively suggesting that even private schoolers, homeschoolers, and anyone else hoping to use those programs for college entrance or credit will not be able to avoid the
umbrella nature of the Common Core.

David Coleman currently travels the country, begging state education departments and universities to join the coalition to support the Common Core and its testing structure. It's not very professional of me to say this, but this guy seriously gives me the creeps.

Pearson

The multinational and multibillion dollar test and education materials corporation, which has gotten off the hook a little too often lately, is one of my most disliked entities in all of this. Pearson is, to exaggerate only slightly, *everywhere*. During the test preparation in New York State and during practice testing and the tests themselves, parents and students noticed something that made them wary: every worksheet and booklet had the Pearson copyright at the bottom of every page. After the tests, parents got pretty upset that they weren't permitted to see the tests in their entirety, since NYSED and Pearson locked them up (or destroyed them) in the name of "security." Despite going through Freedom of Information channels, parents were left without real knowledge of what their kids' tests really even looked like.

In 2011, Pearson created a position called Chief Education Advisor, and excitedly placed Sir Michael Barber into the role. Barber has a history in British government under Tony Blair and was responsible for ensuring that Blair's programs and initiatives were pushed into society effectively. In other words, he was kind of like the Michelle Rhee or David Coleman of Britain, only he was a government employee. In his new role, he finds himself responsible for doing much the same type of work, but for a private, for-profit corporation and on a global scale.[58]

Just prior to joining the Pearson team, Barber worked as McKinsey & Company's Head of Global Education Practice, which is a think tank that purports to specialize in delivery of solutions and ideas to the world's most pressing issues, one of which is education. While at McKinsey, Sir Barber wrote two relatively influential papers that cherry-picked countries and favorable data to suggest that global education challenges can be remedied using technology-delivered learning materials and privatized competitive learning environments. No wonder Pearson wanted him so badly.

Under this leadership, Pearson has truly grown into a global, bloated, and intrusive monopoly in the educational materials-delivery industry. From questionable math textbooks to even more questionable language arts programs and from poorly written standardized tests to the digital concept community, *Pearsonville* (yes, it's a real thing[59]), Pearson has inserted its name into every facet of education. It has even taken the lead in creating technologies that become more than just learning aids, they become our kids' robotic mentors, tracking every grade they earn, every action they take, every course they attempt, and even when those children should be getting up in the morning and what time they should be going to bed.

In the long-term view of things, Pearson envisions a system that follows aptitudes and attitudes, which are tracked starting as young as possible, and guiding those children into programs, special services, and future college and career selections based on achievements, disciplinary and behavior records, determinations of "perseverance, grit, and tenacity," and other data points that are collected consistently throughout the years.

Pearson has been collecting state education contracts for years, and the dollars keep pouring in more aggressively every year. The company recognized early on that the profit motive was very strong with the states' adoption of Common Core and it got to work quickly to start aligning its curricular and testing materials. In some of those programs, Pearson simply "crosswalked" the old standards to the new Common Core and made very minor revisions to textbooks. This certainly saved overhead costs while maximizing profits for the multinational.

In addition to the profit ventures associated with curriculum, Pearson has been awarded major contracts for research, development, and scoring for the two national Common Core testing consortia [Partnership for Assessment of Readiness for College and Careers (PARCC) and the Smarter Balanced

Assessment Consortium (SBAC)], at least one of which schools are required to implement no later than the 2014 – 2015 school year. When students and teachers and schools are ultimately deemed "failures" under these assessments, Pearson also circles like a vulture to swoop down with intervention and remediation materials for all, in order to get those kids to (in David Coleman's words) practice, practice, practice, until they pass the tests. Speaking of David Coleman, his College Board and Pearson are fantastic partners when it comes to finding new and inventive ways to make it more difficult for young high school graduates to get into college. At the same time that the reformers are complaining about college freshman needing remedial courses, Pearson and College Board have joined together to make the college placement test Accuplacer more "rigorous" and CCSS-aligned.[60]

Finally, keep in mind that Pearson is a for-profit corporation, and therefore can do more or less whatever they please in the publicly-funded school system. They continue to advertise heavily for the Common Core and curriculum programs for homeschool and private schools, as well. A private corporation has one primary concern in the global world of business: keeping the profits high and the shareholders happy. Educating students and supporting teachers is a distant secondary (or even tertiary) goal. When Pearson contracts with districts and states to provide professional development and evaluation for teachers, they are not using firm and broad research; they are simply running long, expensive infomercials with the same message as the products being sold on late-night television: this is so easy, an idiot could do it.

The problem is, teachers are not idiots. And we don't like being treated like we are.

Joel Klein

I already introduced this character when talking about Rupert Murdoch. Here's another guy who is generally despised by those who know his game, but he does well to align with powerful and monied interests that like his style. Mostly, I believe they like his law expertise (he's a lawyer by trade) and his cutthroat approach to getting his agenda pushed through. This guy is also dangerous because of the fact that relatively few people even know who he is. I call him the Karl Rove of education reform.

It's strange to know that Klein was the lead prosecutor in the 1998 antitrust case, *United States vs. Microsoft*, and to then realize that he's playing for the same team as Bill Gates. Of course, that case had very little effect on Microsoft, as you surely remember. Klein had some good marks on his past record before apparently being blinded by the money that special interests continued to throw at him. Ironically, as chancellor of New York City in the last decade, he partnered with his old adversary, the Gates Foundation, to fund the opening of charter schools in New York City. He also overstepped his power in 2005, when he fired a teacher's college professor at Columbia University because he didn't like the professor's political views. His actions in NYC made his skills and attitudes attractive to other education investors and reformers.[61]

Before joining Murdoch's wiretapping investigation team and becoming executive vice president of News Corp. in charge of Amplify, Klein helped found Michelle Rhee's astroturf organization, StudentsFirst (rubbing shoulders with David Coleman, perhaps?). He still sits on Rhee's board of directors and still advises policy and agenda items. His tendencies to hire former members of his NYC staff into positions at StudentsFirst and Amplify simply reeks of cronyism in the city government of New York. But, really, is that a surprise to anyone?

There is almost no reform organization out there that isn't wearing Joel Klein like a backpack. He has made himself very comfortable as an advisor to the names above, as well as Jeb Bush, Eli Broad, KIPP, NYC Mayor Bloomberg, and a black book full of others.

Think of Joel Klein as the Karl Rove of education reform. Nobody really likes him, but he works efficiently behind the scenes and gets them what they need.

AFT/NEA

The unions have had a very rough go of things over the past several years. As I mentioned in the introduction, the corporate-run media blitz to discredit and demonize teachers used the unionized professional educator force as a scapegoat, as the enemy of true progress. Without a doubt, the evidence they used to cast a dark shadow on the unions was entirely anecdotal and much of it completely false, but it was successful as a means to reach their goal. From blown-up stories related to pensions, salaries, rubber rooms in New York City, protection of bad teachers, laying off good teachers (okay, that one is personal to me), and generally maintaining a subpar teacher presence, the American public got a very bad vision in their heads of the teachers' unions in this country.

Several local and state school boards starting to create policies and legislation that outlawed or limited union presence and power, and several districts simply chose to cut ties with their union leaders, regardless of protection and collective bargaining laws. As I've also mentioned, this was not some exposé of breaking news; this was a carefully orchestrated and executed plan of action. The move was to get the unions out of the way so corporate interests could move in and do whatever they want to public schools and teachers.

I don't envy the positions of the national union leaders for the National Educators Association (NEA) or the American Federation of Teachers (AFT). This type of national assault and the damage control along the way must have been—and continues to be—draining, strategic, heart wrenching, and just plain exhausting. I don't believe that the leadership handled any of it all that well, however, and now their members are paying a gruesome price.

In a move that smells too much of appeasement, both national unions and their large state chapters have been integral parts of building and agreeing to punitive teacher evaluation policies (based in large part—up to 60%--on student test scores). They also signed the acceptance of adopting and implementing Common Core Standards and the overwhelming testing consortia and data mining companies that come with Race to the Top fund and/or NCLB Waivers.[62]

Amid raucous protests, in 2013, the NEA president chose to ignore up to 35% of his membership in calling for the support of the Common Core and the additional collection of member dues in order to assist with implementation and training. Apparently, the Bill Gates gift was running low, so it came time to start fleecing the masses some more.

AFT has its own marks that make members wary. Randi Weingarten is named on inBloom's website (the private data collection company being used in NYC and piloted in New York State) as an advisor for the governance group for the Shared Learning Collaborative. That group, created by the Council of Chief State School Officers (CCSSO) and funded by Gates Foundation dollars, did some important work, according to inBloom:

> *This group committed significant time to advising those leading the project on the design and long-term governance and future organizational structure.*[63]

In a Twitter conversation with Randi not too long ago, she told me that she was invited to share some ideas, left, and was never invited back. I have enough respect for her to throw her side in here. It's odd, however, that inBloom thought highly enough of her work to leave her name as an important part of that collaborative.

I'm not bashing the national teachers unions, since I still have some hope that the membership will, sooner or later, remove and replace the current leadership after learning of the true allegiances in place. The locals, as you'll read later, have been standing firm against corporate reform and taking newsworthy actions. I expect to see a change soon, amid the embarrassments of national leaders as they realize they probably shouldn't have sold their souls to the monied interests that are trying to hurt their members.

Michelle Rhee

I feel a little bad writing about Michelle Rhee, since I seem to pick on her a lot in my other writings. The thing that bothers me is that she is such a train wreck, I almost feel as though I'm turning into a tabloid writer by continuing to do so. The old cliché, "shooting fish in a barrel," pops into my head every time I write something with her name in the title. However, she is still a relatively formidable and dangerous reformer, so she is going to get her own little section here. I'm also going to spend some time talking about her two sweetheart deals that are working to strip teachers of their professionalism, protections from people like her, and their abilities to teach the students for whom they care for as long as they want.

Michelle Rhee was a teacher of sorts. She graduated as a Teach for America corps member after five weeks of training and started teaching in a very low-performing school in Baltimore,

Maryland. Her kids were unruly, she was stressed to the point of hives, and tests scores plummeted while she was teaching. She took risks that bordered on child abuse and apparently found it funny. Despite the story she told that her second and third year as a teacher were full of success on test scores (years of data that many continue to question as valid), her teaching career can only be classified as a failure.

After that fateful period, Ms. Rhee was somehow able to start The New Teacher Project (TNTP), probably with the backing of corporate reformers who saw a hardliner who could sweetheart their agendas. Regardless, this is where the data addiction most likely took hold. Ms. Rhee's organization evaluates teachers based on student scores, and the teachers in the corps were trained to maximize those scores. The results were nationally recognized, which must have felt really good to Ms. Rhee. When a drug feels good to an addict, you can guess what happens next.

In 2007, Ms. Rhee was named chancellor of the District of Columbia Public Schools and the addiction got worse. Rhee's obsession (and job) was to raise test scores in D.C. and data from those tests became the focus of her career. Other, equally valid evidence of classroom progress and success were no doubt available, but were harder to come by and just didn't feel as good. Raw data gave Michelle Rhee a feeling of power and invincibility.

Michelle Rhee was placed in the spotlight for her hardline and cold approach to teacher and principal evaluations. Her top-down accountability, based on test scores, took control. Left behind were the ideas of professional development, collegiality, personal satisfaction, or love of kids and teaching. Data addiction was the only thing left.

Finally, as seen in *Waiting for Superman* and John Merrow's "The Education of Michelle Rhee," other people around Ms. Rhee began to feel the pain of being around her. She didn't seem to care about anyone but herself. She claimed loudly to care most about the kids, but the talking points didn't match her actions. Firing teachers who really care about their kids doesn't help anyone. Her abuse got out of hand for the people of DC and she was voted out by proxy.[64]

Now, she tours the country (and married a famous mayor) to convince everyone who will pay her or book her that the American school system is a total ruckus and must be revamped. She parrots the nonsense we keep hearing about NAEP, TIMSS, and PISA scores and continues to use anecdotes (which are unverifiable) to sell us on our less-than-average school system. Before she started making a fool out of herself, she did create a pretty successful lobbying company, StudentsFirst, and has funded some very destructive candidates over the years.

StudentsFirst is a group that loves to "educate" those who are relatively ignorant of reality in order to convince them that Michelle's ways are the best ways (firing teachers and principals, closing schools, outlawing unions, propping up politicians and superintendents who wouldn't know what education really looks like if it smacked them upside the head, etc.). It also loves to use celebrity faces and strong heartstrings pulls (again, without any reality or real people) to market and advertise these destructive of those celebrity faces can be found on the d of Directors: Connie Chung, Bill Cosby, and of course, you'll find our friend Joel Klein (see above) and Michelle herself.

Feel free to visit the StudentsFirst "Mission" page at your leisure; it's quite long and basically boils down to this short statement, which I have taken the liberty of paraphrasing and ironizing: *It is our mission to protect the poor children from bad teachers who try to teach them "thinking stuff" instead of how to pass a test. The only way to possibly accomplish this is to close every school and replace it with a private charter filled with good-hearted Teach for America corps members who have no idea how to teach, but will help your student be a master test-taker.*

According to Michelle Rhee, every student deserves a great teacher; and by "great teacher," I mean a Teach for America temporary corps member.

I will continue making fun of Michelle Rhee, because she is a caricature of how ridiculous the education reform movement sounds when they try to sound smart about education. However, I will continue also to counter her lies and misinformation, because they are usually just as dangerous as they are hilarious. Michelle Rhee is a stooge, and StudentsFirst is a rag-tag group of political lobbyists and Teach for America kids who want to play "school reformers." Perhaps the most ridiculous thing that StudentsFirst continues to claim is their "grassroots" beginnings. When Michelle Rhee makes more money for one speaking engagement than I do in a whole year, as she shills to corporate charter managers, hedge fund managers, and other assorted aristocrats, I'm not going to allow her and her army of twenty-something corporate corps members to claim "grassroots" status.

Professional Organizations

There are a few well-known and respected educational organizations that have done great work helping teachers with ongoing development, resource libraries, training, conventions, and assistance for troubled schools. As a teacher, I took great pride in maintaining membership in many of them, not just because of the pad on my resume, but because I knew I had access to fantastic tools and people to guide me as I advanced my practice. At the peak of my resources addiction, I had collected 13 memberships in professional teaching organizations tailored to several specialties, from pedagogy to child development to science and math to special needs and ESL. I felt "armed to the teeth" with all of the knowledge and research a teacher could possibly need. Other than my own, of course.

It was actually a requirement in one of my baccalaureate classes to research and then join at least two professional education organizations. I chose the Association for Supervision and Curriculum Development (ASCD) and the National Council of Teachers of Mathematics (NCTM). The memberships were cheap since I was a student and the resources were impressively numerous. I spent hours upon hours reading, taking notes, and planning how to use many wonderful tools and strategies in my classroom.

I also ordered a few too many books from Solution Tree, which published or promoted the groundbreaking works of Robert and Rebecca DuFour, Robert Marzano, and other rockstars that I thought were the true heroes of public education. That is, until I realized that they had turned their once-revered methods and ideas into ways to turn teachers into data addicts that couldn't teach without spending way too much time following meaningless rubrics and crunching numbers from standardized tests and common assessments.

The DuFours pushed the idea of the professional learning community (PLC), which started out as a nifty program to start getting teachers out of isolation and talking to each other about best practices. But, like with just about anything else to come out recently, it ended up turning into a menacing barrier to effective practice. The PLC, in my well-researched opinion, has become a bane to teacher creativity and individuality and has turned the academic environment into one that revolves around hard data. Teachers don't like this stuff. Not just because it's dry and boring and relatively useless, but because it automatically reduces our students to numbers and ranks. We know our kids; we don't need constant data streams of test scores being fed to us to know how to teach them.

What all of this hype and propaganda led to, basically, is an environment where administrators must follow a complex rubric to evaluate their teachers and where teachers must sacrifice significant portions of their planning times to prepare tests statements in the name of "accountability." ASCD, Solution Tre and many others have rolling marketplaces for resources that are sold as important tools to help teachers get ready for Common Core, turn PLCs into true data-lovin' meetings, and how to use the very limited information from common assessments to decide what to bore your kids with next.

Sorry for the cynicism, but that's pretty much how it's all starting to look.

Additionally and dishearteningly, many of the subject-specific and subgroup-specific organizations have seemed to jump on board the Common Core Initiative. I want to point to the National Council of Teachers of Mathematics (NCTM), National Science Teachers Association (NSTA), the Council of Administrators of Special Education (CASE), and the Council for Exceptional Children (CEC), since I know that there are significant numbers among their ranks who dissent and don't recognize the Common Core as a means to fully educate the children in their classrooms. These organizations once did a service to teachers who looked to them for assistance in creating the best public school experience possible for their students; now, teachers are being led to believe that standardized learning is the way to go and too many of the resources, tools, and training events are shilling for the expansion of corporate reform.[65]

So, why? Why would previously esteemed organizations sell their souls, so to speak, to jump on this chaotic mess of unsupported reform? I'm sure I don't even need to answer that

·s: B-i-l-l G-a-t-e-s. Let me pick on ASCD a

、.ᴜ that ASCD has nothing left to offer professional ..ᴜrs and leaders, because that would be dishonest of me. I still come across articles written by respected and very intelligent, experienced practitioners who have much to share. As a former member and subscriber of ASCD and its publications, I have learned many tricks, methods, and ideas from the authors of those articles. However, a recent news tip out of Atlanta shows something that we all should have seen coming, and another reason to boycott such organizations as those listed above, other than their signatures on the Common Core Standards.

Atlanta Public Schools just signed into a partnership with ASCD, which has been contracted to provide the district with professional development resources, tools, and people. Atlanta, just like many other districts, has been scrambling for ways to make Common Core work in their schools using their own overburdened human resources, and are finding the costs and the hours hard to cover. Not because educators aren't intelligent and dedicated enough to do the work, but because the standards and the demands that come with them were sprung onto districts with tight deadlines, no compensation, and bad material—not to mention, the standards themselves cannot be changed or deleted, and several teachers either can't or won't create curricula aligned to standards that they feel are inappropriate for their kids. Several other districts have reported that the resistance to implementing flawed, poorly written, and unsupported standards is severe enough to put the brakes on getting the modules (i.e. scripts) written in time to be prepared for the national tests (also flawed, poorly written, and not supported by research).

So, professional organizations like the ASCD have taken on the task to name themselves experts and sell their wares to "struggling" districts. Again, it's all about the money and the race to be the most popular Common Core resource repository.

This, of course, is nothing new. Once the standards were released to schools, there was mass movement by individual teachers, consultants, companies, and organizations to be the first on the scene with snake oil to sell. ASCD was towards the front of that line, especially with administrator buy-in and training resources.

With Gates funding, ASCD attempted to sell its customers on the Common Core with questionable research (how can you research something that hasn't happened yet?) and broad, new terminology with new definitions that were shaped as needed. ASCD willfully ignored real research and evidence in order to support what the cash told them to support. There can be no remaining reason to support this sellout non-profit corporation as a reliable or reputable educational organization. They have decided to become the American arm of the Pearson Corporation—selling poor resources, based on shoddy research, for the pursuit of wealth. They are not alone, though. Check the organization names I listed above and be skeptical of their research and their purposes. Be skeptical of any organization or person who wants to sell the magic potion for Common Core success.

National Media

This will be the shortest part of this chapter, since there has been hardly any media buzz around national education policy, Race to the Top, or Common Core. The only consistently run story I can recall is the one about America always being dumber in reading, math, and science than the rest of the world. This, of course, is the echo of voices from several of the people and groups I just discussed.

What's frustrating is the lack of coverage from "the other side" (our side) of the education issue. There have been some notable attempts by MSNBC's Chris Hayes and Ed Schultz, as well as PBS's John Merrow (whose work centers on Michelle Rhee), Glenn Beck, and a few misguided segments by Fox News's Megyn Kelly and Sean Hannity (who mostly focused on Common Core).

There has been virtually no coverage of school closings or teacher layoffs in Philadelphia or Chicago, no coverage of the Seattle test boycotts, no coverage of the test score debacle in New York State, no coverage of Los Angeles USD's fight for autonomy, and no investigation whatsoever into any of the power players in this chapter. None. Even the few spots on National Public Radio about Common Core have been spiteful of those fighting it (which comes to no real surprise, considering the amounts of money that NPR receives from the Gates and Walton Foundations, among others).

Grassroots movements like the education reform resistance get used to having their voices silence or demonized in the national mainstream media. That's why we must grow in numbers and influence, and make our voices louder than the clutter that is hijacking the airwaves.

So, there's my totally non-inclusive lists of those who have chosen to either create or support the education reforms that are currently causing the foundation of our envied public school system to crack and falter. As you can see, billionaires have taken their roles in American society into new, more aggressive directions, as they now seek to control the way we advance into the future. And it's for their own benefit, not ours. There are many strategies on the corporate table to grow our next generation into the workforce that they desire, as they attempt to stifle organization of workers (including teachers), creativity of potential competitors, and the critical faculties of the citizens they seek to control. They have big plans and are throwing big money behind those plans.

You what sounds almost worse than all of that? When all of their big plans and grand schemes are either abandoned or overthrown, this big-money club will likely do what billionaires and corporations always do when their ideas fall apart. Remember Enron? Remember the housing bubble? When the walls come down on a big corporate scheme, the leaders and owners pack up their money and assets (which are sheltered in some offshore accounts, anyway), walk quietly away from the mess, and wash their hands of it all. No accountability, no responsibility.

This time, however, they aren't putting our homes or our jobs or our health at risk. This time they've gone way too far. They are targeting our kids. The desire to take over the education system for profit and planning has been around for quite a while. The plan has been built and the strategies are in place. They are fairly ingenious in their evil, and they rely on Americans staying busy, quiet, and in constant conflict, as I discussed in the introduction.

The next chapter will explore one of those strategies in more depth, as well as visit some of the others currently at play.

The Baby and the Bathwater

CHAPTER

3

The Baby and the Bathwater

"One test of the correctness of educational procedure is the happiness of the child."

– Maria Montessori

Race to the Top is the program that allows government oversight and authority in cooperation with the corporate reform movement. In other words, it keeps schools, districts, and states quiet and compliant so that the investors and reformers discussed in the last chapter can work their magic. Often, during debates about high-stakes testing, the Common Core Standards, and the other pieces of the big puzzle (data mining, common curriculum, etc.), you can expect someone to throw out the following statement:

Don't throw out the baby with the bathwater!

The suggestion here is that we can get rid of the things that are blatantly harmful to our children and the education system at large, but there are some good things in there that we should just leave alone. This stance shows that some people (perhaps *most* people) hold a misunderstanding regarding the cohesiveness of Race to the Top programs that were required to win money, and which have been given life even in states that didn't win. According to folks who make this statement, the "baby" in this scenario is the body of common, national content standards we know as the Common Core. The bathwater, which is contaminated with bad policies such as testing programs and funding schemes, needs to be changed out.

Personally, I hate the "baby and bathwater" adage, because it paints a picture of some precious portion of the whole rotten stew. It attempts to sell the idea that the Common Core is somehow worth saving. It attempts to ignore a verifiable truth about the whole mess: the Common Core Standards, the high-stakes testing, and the data collection to support the growing privatization schemes are inextricably linked. Let's talk about that.

The Baby

I'm going to give the Common Core State Standards (CCSS) their own big section here, which I can use to argue against some of the wonderful things said about them (there aren't many) and to discuss some of the things that make them a rotten and destructive force in the 21st century in the United States. Or, anywhere, really. I have engaged in many debates with teachers, principals, union leaders, and others who have defended them to the point where I just finally had to go to bed. What was depressing was the fact that, in every single debate, my opposing colleagues had included several of the exact same talking points that I consistently read in early pro-CCSS literature. They were also the same talking points I had heard over and over again in teacher development sessions, in which we were "trained" to love and teach the Core. They were the same talking points and beatitudes that I presented to parents when I was "cheerleading" for them a year and a half ago.

Let me tell you the overall philosophical objection I have to nationally common content standards, and then I will focus on the standards themselves.

Diane Ravitch, not too long ago, wrote a blog post about her stance regarding the Common Core State Standards, basically suggesting that she could not support them because of their lack of evidence of effectiveness.[66] In that article, she explained that she must remain agnostic, rather than supportive, of the Common Core since it has not been field tested or otherwise vetted by substantial research. I also don't support the Common Core for her reasons, but I'm not "agnostic" about them. I have seen more evidence over the past few months than is needed to support my original idea that the Common Core State Standards make up the *foundation* of the drive for corporate education reform. Sitting just atop that foundation, Race to the Top creates the funding and the mandates for testing and student data mining. High-stakes testing is an industry unto itself, and that testing lends data to the collection systems that are currently attempting to lead our kids into preset futures. Finally, using the data-driven failure model of more "rigorous" standards and harder tests rises the ultimate plan for privatization of the public school system.

One idea that I keep hearing repeated is, almost word for word, "I have no problem with the standards themselves, but the implementation was totally wrong." I nod my head in agreement, since the implementation was obviously a total mess. There were simply too many state chiefs and other school leaders rushing to get to the top—trying to make their constituencies appear ahead of the curve—regardless of the outcomes or the effects on students. After all, there was a deadline to meet and money to win!

And the only call to resistance was a plea to delay the high-stakes measures aligned to the standards, and the ultimate decisions based on those measures, until everyone had a chance to get them implemented.

Several state chiefs responded to that resistance call—which was mostly made by national and state union leaders—by saying that we've all had enough time already to get settled and there won't be any more grace periods. It took an executive statement by Arne Duncan, himself, to get permission to "put the brakes on the stakes," as Randi Weingarten, president of the American Federation of Teachers, would say.[67] Why the U.S. Secretary of Education gets to tell us when to evaluate our teachers and schools based on a national curriculum makes my eyebrows raise a bit.

So, a group of teachers across America (but, by no means, the majority of all teachers) started parroting the words of their union leaders. The standards aren't the problem; the implementation was bad. Some teachers who *do* oppose the standards hope that if we can stop the standardized testing, the Common Core will simply fade away, like all the other "fads."

This is where the division among teachers shows up loudly and clearly. Some call for the end of high-stakes testing, or at least a moratorium. Some call for the withdrawal from Race to the Top, knowing that the funding states are receiving from the Federal Department of Education isn't enough to cover the costs associated with meeting the requirements. Still others call for the return of control to local entities, such as districts or regions. I support all of those.

Here, though, I'd like to discuss the idea that the Common Core State Standards are not simply a fad and they are not a secondary or tertiary piece of the overall program. Using the well-known "train has left the station" allegory, I suggest that the standards are the rails upon which the train races. High-stakes testing, which is used for teacher evaluations and school ranking, drives the locomotive. The cargo being hauled behind the tests includes everything else in the program: curriculum being sold for profits, charter school operators looking for the next dying school, Broad Academy superintendents looking for the next job, data miners pulling student and teacher information into central storage, and a fancy car in which the corporate reformers sit and sip their fancy drinks and count their profits.

We can get our leaders to ease up on the testing and we can get laws passed that keep our kids' privacy intact. But, it's a sure thing that those victories will be temporary, since the corporate "reformers" will always seek to rebuild a new structure—a new train—on top of the CCSS foundational tracks (billionaires seeking profits simply don't give up that easily). The foundation has to be removed (or weakened to the point of uselessness) in order to slow the efforts of corporations wanting to "reform" education for the sake of profits–now and in the future. The trains that are built for corporate reformers must be denied the rails on which to run.

This is going to be a little tougher, since so many politicians, teachers, and education leaders have bought into the idea that the CCSS are relatively benign, if not beneficial. That's probably slightly untrue though, since I think that educational professionals are mostly thinking about the things that have been said to them, or the things that are discussed in school meetings, professional development sessions, and other protected venues. They haven't yet had the time to look more deeply or the exposure to alternative media sources.

There are two, oft-repeated mantras associated with people who oppose the overwhelming numbers of high-stakes, standardized tests and the damage they are doing to our classrooms, yet support the idea of the Common Core Standards.

Here's Mantra #1:

The Common Core State Standards are not the problem; the "rollout" (or implementation) is the problem. They came out too fast and the testing should have waited.

This is what Randi Weingarten of the American Federation of Teachers keeps repeating and what many others seem to misunderstand. Unfortunately, it's simply not true. This little statement is many times followed by Mantra #2:

> *There is some merit to the Common Core State Standards, and they are theoretically sound. We just need better materials and more time to get them implemented correctly.*

Let's spend a little bit of time getting to know why these two statements are both meaningless, if not dangerous. And instead of rambling on and repeating some of my older writing, I would like to try something a little more creative.

Let's compare the Common Core State Standards to a Snickers chocolate bar. Yes, a *Snickers bar.*

Look at Mantra #1 again, but this time, we'll change "Common Core State Standards" to read "Snickers bars." We'll pretend that the "rollout" is a new mandate by the state education department that Snickers bars be the main course of all school breakfasts and lunches–*for all kids.* Why? Because some schools are not doing a very good job of putting enough protein into their students' diets. We all know protein is good for brain and muscle development, and we all know that peanuts have protein. How can our kids into a good college without protein and brain development? We'll use Snickers because they're tasty and will encourage student consumption.[68]

During the program, every so often, the state will take blood tests from the students to check their protein levels. The blood test results will be stored in a database, which will determine college readiness, based on the correlation between protein-blood levels and brain development. If the levels are too low, the cafeteria staff will receive "consequences" and will be enrolled in a "mandatory development program." If the levels look good, the cafeteria staff will receive "incentives," including pay-for-performance awards.

Sound silly? Well, that's because it is. But just like the Common Core—an untested, unproven method of trying to boost "student achievement" based on two sets of poorly-written subject standards—the Snickers plan has no realistic hope of readying everyone for college and careers. Instead of blaming the policy or the standards for being failed attempts, we are hell-bent on blaming the *teachers,* who had nothing to do with those standards or their implementation. (Side note: there is more evidence supporting protein's role in brain development than there is evidence for the Common Core's ability to ready everyone for college.)

Oh, and everyone *has* to eat their Snickers portions, even if they're allergic to peanuts or milk or whatever. That's just how it is. Some accommodations will be provided, as needed, but there is no "opt out" provision to get out of eating the Snickers or taking the blood tests. Those who encourage their kids to "refuse" the blood tests must not want to know if their children are healthy.

Okay. On to Mantra #2. I once alluded to the idea that there is one, and only one, part of the Common Core State Standards that I like. I like the eight "Mathematical Practices" because they are not standards. They are not content or subject standards like the rest of the national curriculum tries to be. They are *habits*. There's nothing wrong with asking teachers to help their students practice good habits, but I also don't know very many teachers *who weren't already doing that.*

So, yes, a part of the Common Core Standards do have some merit: the part that doesn't contain any standards. If you pick through the content standards, you will also find some merit. There's no doubt about that. Does that mean the entire thing should be kept in place and practice? Lots of people like to use that "baby and bathwater" analogy to suggest that we shouldn't throw out all of the standards just because there are some that are developmentally inappropriate or out of place.

Why can't we throw out the bathwater and the baby, especially if the baby isn't a baby at all? If there is no evidence that the CCSS as a whole will lead to individual readiness for life, then there is no reason to keep it in play or practice, even if there is "some merit." Not to mention, strict content standards systems like the CCSS automatically create a "factory model" of education. You know, the 19th century system we've been trying to break away from all these years? The system that *teachers* were finally leading us away from, until they were silenced and contained by corporate money and interests?

Does our Snickers program have "some merit?" Sure it does! Snickers bars have peanuts! And, well, relatively low sodium. And a great ad campaign!

The point is, despite the silliness, my Snickers allegory is trying to make an important point. We have pushed a national set of content standards onto every child with the intent of getting them to compete against each other for spots in the future corporate hierarchy. We have focused on a few points of "merit" without taking a good look at the harmful side effects of this system of reform. We have created a one-size-fits-all education system that is currently harmful to many kids, as it increases so-called achievement gaps and dropout rates, kills creativity and critical thought, and chases effective teachers from the melee. We have rolled out an entire system that has no evidence base, no consideration for what it means to be a developing human in a complex environment, and no real thought about the long term consequences for our kids.

My new school diet would certainly do great things for the company that makes Snickers, but the damage to our kids and our economy would be disastrous. Much the same of the Common Core State Standards.

The CCSS were not designed (contrary to what we were told to believe) by teachers, education experts, or university professors. Their creation and implementation were only led by "states" in the sense that some representatives from state coalitions gave the go-ahead to David Coleman, Bill McCollum, and Achieve, Inc., to get busy with their work.[69] Once the standards were drafted, small teams of "advisory" teachers were consulted to read and comment. There is no documentation to suggest that these teachers were chosen based on any type of merit or if their comments (if any) were considered in further drafts of those standards. The simple fact seems to be that the CCSS were written and accepted by a very small number of people, who are not identifiable as educators by any definition of the word. Yet, I keep hearing good educators use corporate talking points to defend them.

When you take a good look at the standards, in the way they were intended to be read, you begin to realize that there are some fundamental problems and some very dangerous implications for the future. For instance, knowing that the standards were "backwards mapped" (which means the architects started with a vision of a "perfect" high school graduate, and then created standards from 12th grade down to Kindergarten in order to reach that ideal), it makes sense that reading the standards starting at the Kindergarten level and working your way up would be a logical way of analyzing them. It's also a good idea to choose one strand and follow that particular strand all the way to 12th grade to watch what changes, since the standards are also "progressive," meaning each strand gets more complex as the years go by.

When reading through the Kindergarten standards for either math or English-language arts (or both) the first striking fact is how many there are (I count 25 math standards and 80 ELA standards). The designers of the website for the Common Core (corestandards.org) did well to break all of the standards up by grade level and again by domain and strand. That way, only a few standards show up per click. But, if you list all of them on one page, you realize that Kindergarten just became something different from what we're used to. It has become—what's the word they love to use?—"rigorous."

Let me take a brief aside, here, and then I'll get back to the early elementary standards. Let's talk rigor for moment.

Rigor is another word that's been flung around like the newest and must-have fad in education (I was going to reference baboons here, but that might have been childish). Teachers cannot design a lesson or an activity or field trip without the required "rigor" being included in there somewhere. They usually even have to use the word itself. That poses the same problem as "college and career ready:" nobody has any consensus on what it means, much less what it's supposed to look like, yet it has become part of every single conversation and piece of propagandized information.

Rigor is everywhere now: rigorous standards, rigorous curriculum, rigorous tests, rigorous teacher evaluations, rigorous behavior plans. I could go on. Most professional educators would agree with the definition used by Barbara Blackburn, which suggests that rigor is "creating an environment in which each student is expected to learn at high levels, each student is supported...and each student demonstrates learning at high levels."[70] I would add that not every student's learning or demonstration has to look the same. (I will also add that Blackburn fits snugly into chapter two with all of the other corporate shills, and I think that her definition has different implications for her than what most professionals teachers believe.) Rigor should be another individualized aspect of learning. Students should be guided to determine what their own rigorous learning and productivity look like.

To suggest that the Common Core State Standards are rigorous is to grossly misuse the term in an educational sense. Common content standards simply cannot provide that type of environment, even if they promise to. That's not what the sellers of the standards mean, anyway, as far as I can see. Reading through the standards, you can see that rigor doesn't mean any of what Ms. Blackburn suggests. It simply means what the Merriam-Webster online dictionary defines: "the quality of being unyielding or inflexible." Or, perhaps this definition: "a condition of making life difficult, challenging, or uncomfortable."

Merryl Tisch, of the New York Board of Regents, would agree and praise the latter definition—she certainly praised the New York end-of-year assessments for their rigor, even as more and more reports of crying, vomiting, and failing kids poured in. Rigorous assessments mean nothing more than longer, more difficult, and poorly adapted for the grade levels for which they are designed.

Finally, the rigor in teacher evaluations is a misnomer to end all misnomers. There is no rigor in teacher evaluations; there is only an increasing set of hoops to jump through, year after year, to make it look more and more difficult to prove themselves effective. This is not rigor; this is, quite simply, gaming the system and cheating teachers.

Okay, let's get back to the "rigorous" Kindergarten standards.

I'm finally going to partially offer my answer to the question that clever Common Core supporters keep asking me:

"*Which* standards do you think are inappropriate?"

Fine. Here we go. Everything in this section is based on the notes I kept from my master's program, as I researched and read through thousands of pages of child development and cognition research journals and performed my own research, as well. No, I don't have sources to cite, other than my own notes. That's okay, though, because this book is not an academic journal.

I'll start with mathematics.

Let's skip the counting and cardinality standards, because I've seen those skills being taught in Kindergarten for as long as anyone can remember. The "Comparing Numbers" strand is also reasonable, although I question whether or not Kindergartners are cognitively prepared to compare cardinal numbers the same way they can compare concrete quantities of actual objects. They can be trained to tell you which number is bigger, but some of them will not be able to grasp the symbolism behind their answers for another year or so.

Then, we have addition and subtraction. Addition is a relatively simple concept for young children and tends to happen naturally as a concrete skill. Even toddlers know the concept of *more*, and will begin to quantize what they mean or what they want by age three or four. By age four, children can truly understand the idea that adding two items to a collection of two results in a new quantity of four. However, they will not be able to automatically understand the symbolism of $2 + 2 = 4$. This is an abstract skill that must be equated to the concrete reality, over and over, and when the child is cognitively prepared. A cognitive ability, known as "conserving," is needed to do symbolic addition, and children develop this ability at different rates. Conserving is the ability to hold a number in one's head while using other numbers to change the quantity. In studies that span decades, it's shown that the *average* five-year-old can develop their ability to conserve to about the number 13, while counting, and to the number 8, while thinking.

The Common Core Standards attempt to bypass this important research by making sure that students can add both ways within 10. *All students.* This may be doable, but then the standards go on to demand overly-demanding addition tasks for Kindergarteners. For example, decomposition of number into two different addition problems is entirely too abstract for most Kindergarteners to grasp, much less make sense of or find relevance in. While many of them may be able to do it because they've memorized and copied it enough, they are not cognitively prepared to understand the meaning. This is a concept best saved for the 7- or 8-year-old group, or maybe even later. Putting this skill into the early standards is simply an attempt to experiment with pushing algebra into Kindergarten, and it's not only inappropriate, it's also completely unnecessary.

There is only one standard that applies to subtraction, which is also too abstract: symbolic equations (e.g. $5 - 3 = 2$). Kindergarteners can certainly grasp that if someone removes three of their five pennies, they only have two left. But the conserving abilities of Kindergarteners makes abstract subtraction incredibly frustrating and left to memorization rather than understanding, which doesn't do the kids any good.

This is a pattern that is emerging in the new education movement, which is paved by the Common Core Standards. It's assumed that young children can do more and learn faster than they used to, which contradicts research that has been conducted for a long time. The truth is, five-year-old brains—and the innate capabilities and developments within—have remained pretty static over the years. The only thing to change is our expectation of their abilities. This cultural shift in *adult* thinking is stressful and unfair to the children we push beyond their capabilities.

This thinking is, unfortunately, bolstered by academic research that suggests that young children can score slightly higher on standardized math tests when they are taught more advanced concepts. This leads to the idea that training Kindergarten students to perform on certain higher-level math skills leads to more learning. However, the studies do not support that idea, since the research is incomplete. Longitudinal data from student test scores have not yet been analyzed. However, I see no conclusive support coming from these studies anyway, since the standardized tests do not measure skills beyond memorizing, regurgitating, and taking standardized tests. In other words, if you can train someone to do something enough times and for long enough, they can probably do it better than those without training, even if it means nothing.

Next comes place value (ones, tens, hundreds, and so on) and geometry. Place value is a relatively difficult concept, as evidenced by classroom grades and surveys from several teachers in elementary grades. Historically, learning about place value and the decomposition of numbers into ones, tens, and so on, has been a third-grade skill—second-grade at the earliest. However, some children struggle with it as late as fifth or sixth grade. That's because not only is it a pretty abstract idea, but there isn't a whole lot of relevance for place value in a young kid's world.

Geometry can be both highly concrete and very abstract. Kindergarteners normally show up to their first day of class knowing the names of basic shapes, regardless of orientation or size, but that's where the average commonality ends. Not all students are ready to describe shapes based on sides or angles, nor are many of them ready to compare shapes to other shapes based on those attributes. Many students have difficulty drawing shapes with single lines (e.g. drawing triangles is more difficult to master with a single line than rectangles and circles). Finally, using basic shapes to compose new, larger or different shapes is also an abstract skill that students struggle with, even with the use of manipulatives and trial-and-error.

The problem with the Common Core Standards in math is that they were written to assume that skills outside of cognitive range can be accomplished using strict mental training, use of concrete objects to understand abstract ideas, rote memorization, and students' reflection of their own work. The question, "How do you know?" has become synonymous with Kindergartener frustration (even temper tantrums) during homework time. When a child's cognitive readiness is ignored, and their biological and psychological capabilities are surpassed in expectation of completing a task, asking her how she knows the answer is right is salt in the wound. A student can't tell you *how* they know when they aren't really sure that they *know* in the first place. In mathematics, the most important part of teaching (or developing standards) is understanding age-appropriate skills and developmental readiness. The Common Core Standards fall flat in this regard.

So, what about the English-language arts (ELA) standards? There are many more of them, and they have the same, basic folly. There are some that are reasonable (and also not new) and some that attempt to do more before it's time. For example, the standards for literature are basically fine, except for the one lonely standard that asks 5-year-olds to read with "purpose and understanding." These are children who are barely starting to work on their fluency by simply attempting to sound easy words out and recognize their first "sight words" (words that are difficult to sound out and are therefore recognized, or memorized). Reading with purpose and understanding is not only a vague description of a standard, but also, in many cases, fully outside of the ability of a five-year-old reader.

Where it starts to get nutty is the "informational text" domain. Although most of these standards do start off "with prompting and support," many of them are still outside of a Kindergartener's schema, even if there were enough teachers to effectively offer that support (which there aren't). One standard asks young children to find reasons that an author uses to support points that are made in a text. I've seen this strategy used in storytelling, but asking these kids to back up an author's writing is problematic, at best. First of all, it again relies on the same skill that is still developing in math: conserving. Kindergarteners would need to conserve items from text in order to meet that standard. Several of them would be able to conserve one or two main ideas, but not several specific points. Many would be so busy trying to decode the words, that they wouldn't have the mindset to remember details from the text.

In order for reading comprehension and analysis to happen, *fluency* must be attained. It's very apparent that the Common Core wants to see both happen at the same time, which is unrealistic. Some have come back at me by saying that the comprehension part of the standards comes into play when an adult is reading to them. I understand that, but then we have the conserving problems rising up again. And remember, these standards are going to be tested starting in 2014 in Kindergarten. How do you test this?

In any case, of course I believe that Kindergarten teachers should definitely read to their classes and ask guiding, predictive, and review questions about the texts. The program now is new, however, in that every student is being expected to show some level of "proficiency" in meeting those standards. Again, even if there were enough teachers to go around and assess each kid authentically (which there aren't), it's unrealistic to expect that all kids will be on the same track at the same time.

Another specific standard that is not Kindergarten-appropriate states that students should be able to "demonstrate understanding of the organization and basic features of print." Even if this standard weren't incredibly vague, we must again remember that we are teaching young children who are just beginning. Most of them will be starting or continuing the guided act of printing letters in practice. To understand the organization, structure, and features of print sounds odd for this age group. There are actually several standards throughout ELA that call for Kindergarteners to have command or understanding of things for which their brains are simply not prepared and for which there really is no relevance.

Phonics is also introduced early. Syllables are something that some Kindergarteners might be able to hear at this age, but by no means all of them. Syllable recognition, counting, blending, and segmenting are second- or third-grade skills, historically. To try to get Kindergarteners to be proficient in these skills is frustrating and, again, simply an act of training rather than learning. Also in this category are recognizing and spelling using long and short vowel sounds and associating those with new and different words.

The domain that really starts to worry me is the *writing* domain. Kindergarteners have been successful in trying to compose emergent sentences or phrases using their own thoughts, creativity, memories, or reflections. What Common Core attempts to do is start research-based and text-dependent writing way too early. This domain is one of those things that makes me (and many others) ask, *why?* Seriously, what's the rush? And what evidence is there that starting at this level, where children are still learning to write the names of people they love and sentences about their puppies, will somehow prepare them and give them a head start for the future? The first writing standard asks students to basically do a book report and, second, write an informative text. But that's not all! Next, they are expected to read each other's texts (or have them read aloud), critique and offer suggestions, and then respond to questions and suggestions from their peers in order to strengthen their writing.

It sounds so wonderful, like a group of tiny scholars! I've actually heard teachers tell me how wonderful it sounds and how exciting it's going to be. None of those teachers, however, have been Kindergarten teachers. Middle school and high school ELA teachers love the idea of making five-year-old research, write, back up their writing, critique each other, and then revise. I remember hearing about this in one of my middle school Common Core professional development sessions and feeling slightly sick (and angry). Many of my colleagues in ELA were also visibly upset; others, mostly younger teachers, were thrilled. Somehow, the buy-in suggests that Common Core will prepare upcoming middle schoolers to be totally proficient and ready to meet all secondary standards.

I don't think it will make any positive difference at all. If it does, it will affect kids in different ways and will probably expand the already wide spectrum in writing ability for those middle-level kids. Every Kindergarten teacher with whom I've spoken, many of whom have tried this domain, have told me it's ridiculous. Most of them even use that exact word. These are young children. This is not how they learn to write.

Finally, the *language* domain.

This is where the conventions of English are listed, almost one-by-one, of which Kindergartners are expected to have "command" by the end of the year. Teachers know what that word means. Command is the ability to conjure up skills and processes that have been mastered and are available for use when the student needs them. These conventions, of which students should have command, are grammar, punctuation, spelling, phonetics, suffixes and prefixes, synonyms and antonyms, and "shades" of verbs. I wish I were making this up. It's in there. How did even non-educators think that this was a good domain for Kindergarten? Did they not see the huge leap from "asking about unknown words in a text," to having "command" of the English language when writing or speaking?

Perhaps I'm being specific or picky where they may be some flexibility, but the fact remains that we are pushing skills and knowledge into a level where they don't yet comfortably belong. And for no reason that is supported by any research. The research in opposition to early elementary CCSS continues to grow.[71]

There were reportedly no early elementary teachers or specialists on the development team for the Common Core State Standards, and it's readily apparent just by reading them. Many Kindergarten teachers (and other early learning specialists) have made observations and statements that can be summed up as such:

Jean Piaget and Lev Vygotsky have been replaced
by Bill Gates and David Coleman

What about middle and high school? Many teachers in these levels tell me that they are pleased with the skills that are prescribed to grades six through twelve, stating that they are responsible for getting students to think more deeply about the texts they read and getting them used to using text triangulation and other media as evidence for their writing and speaking. Some teachers have even reporting seeing their own practice becoming so much more impressive, thanks to the CCSS. My response is, generally, that I would wish for these professionals to give themselves some credit for their own best practices. After asking some of those teachers what they were doing prior to the standards, they would either give a vague answer in order to maintain credit to the standards, or they would stop and realize that their new talents were simply a matter of professional growth and research, and had very little to do with these new standards.

I will concede that middle school is where the standards probably feel the most benign or beneficial. The math and ELA standards seem to be more developmentally appropriate for those middle levels, so teachers within that range with often rave about them. The problem, however, is that these teachers have not yet had a chance to see the effects of the early elementary standards on the kids that rise from fifth grade (or whenever kids reach those middle levels). You see, the standards are linearly progressive, meaning each strand becomes more complex with every year that passes. So, kids are expected to master the current year's standards so that they are able to pick up with the new, more complex standards and continue working toward "proficiency."

What if a student doesn't show proficiency at the end of the year? Either they move on, without the prerequisite skills for the following year, or they are forced to attend summer school (in order to pass a test), or they are forced to sacrifice elective choices in lieu of "extra help" classes. Or, they are held back and required to repeat a grade or class. According to David Coleman, students who don't master the standards during the year will "practice [them] again and again and again and again, so there's a chance they can finally do that level of work."[72] Only a non-educator with a god-complex would say such a thing.

Regardless, some children will find themselves perpetually behind, since they may not be developmentally "average," or they will find themselves in a constant rut, never getting to explore other offerings of a good education, since they're always stuck in remedial and response-to-intervention classes. It goes without saying, then, that students who struggle in ELA and math will not enjoy the same enrichments in school as their more highly-performing peers. Research has shown over and over for a long time how important those exploratory choices are, and stripping them for the sake of mastery of content standards will most certainly have deleterious effects for those students who struggle.

The Baby and the Bathwater

It's also odd that so many high school teachers support the Common Core Standards. Standardized learning and same-pace curricula are probably the most damaging in secondary levels. This should be the time when we're ensuring that students are proficient in the skills that will make them successful in general life and in our American society. Using a set of rigid standards as the most important guide in the program will push aside the priorities of helping to develop our middle and high school students as they grow into responsible, intelligent, curious, skeptical, and thinking adults. Many claim that the CCSS help to accomplish just that; I disagree.

The Common Core has very specific academic skills that are geared toward preparing community college students, and they don't do a very good job of that. (I don't buy the "career" part of "college and career ready;" it assumes that every career must have the same build up to the same terminal set of skills. That's not only completely unrealistic, it's also silly. The world changes too fast to makes that type of prediction.) Our students need to be ready for whatever comes around, which means having a well-rounded education for which they, themselves, are mostly responsible for pursuing. Common Core Standards are just a form of hand-holding our high school students through the things corporate America expects of them, without allowing them to truly explore the world and their options.

Last point: I'm tired of hearing how the Common Core Standards are finally going to teach our kids how to *think critically*. For one thing, the people who promote the standards based on this premise do not understand what thinking critically means or looks like (which means that maybe those people should start learning how to think critically, no?). There has been a debate in academic circles for quite some about whether or not critical thinking can actually be taught or if it's a skill that simply starts to develop over the ages.

I will not delve into the research, but I will suggest this: critical thinking is a skill that can be *modeled*. In other words, when children have adults or peers, who are efficient critical thinkers, model their own thoughts and mindsets out loud, and when children then start to practice those things out loud, critical thinking becomes a development that is ongoing. The Common Core Standards attempt to sell deep reading, text references, and triangulation as critical thinking, but I won't accept any of that as the only means to the end. First of all, there is no end—critical thinking is a skill that is always being developed. Second, a person can practice the skills that the standards prescribe and still never become a critical thinker.

Good teachers have been working on and using best practices for critical thinking for far longer than content standards even existed. When you hear folks say that they "really like the Common Core Standards because they focus on and prioritize critical thinking," tell them, "No, they don't. Teachers do."

A quick summary. From Kindergarten to fourth or fifth grade, the standards are wildly outside of the research regarding child development and cognitive ability. As soon as

Kindergartners walk in the door, they are set up (and expected) to falter or fail. Middle school standards don't seem as unreasonable, mostly because students and the standards have become more in tune to the "fewer, deeper, higher" motto by then. However, it also forces teachers to leave out several standards, since time usually runs out before all of the standards are taught. Since the standards are invariably linked to the testing and accountability systems that were designed for them, failure is also commonplace there. In high school, we will start to see the ever-widening achievement gaps, which CCSS were supposed to alleviate. Worst of all, the high school standards will cause the narrowing of the curricula that so many are concerned with. True learning and exploration of the future at the expense of narrow and rigid content standards. It just doesn't make any sense in this time in history.

Our children are not common and they are not standard. Common national standards simply do not fit the research and they do not fit the realities inherent in teaching, learning, and development of children. Kids do things at different times. To suggest that getting every state on board to do the same things at the same times will change that is purely and completely unrealistic. Not to mention, dangerous.

Standard Curricula and High-Stakes Testing

I wrote a relatively long chapter in *Children of the Core* about high-stakes testing and its use in evaluating teaching and learning. To quickly summarize:

1. *Standardized testing is based on "junk science."* There is no evidence to suggest that students learn more or achieve at higher levels by prepping for or taking standardized tests.

2. *The experts (educators) aren't making the tests or the policies regarding testing.* Therefore, the tests themselves are often poorly designed and are not being used for pedagogical purposes.

3. *Teachers can't use these expensive tests.* Teachers are qualified and well-trained to create, administer, and use varied types of assessments to gauge their students' developments and achievements. They, in turn, use these assessments to guide what happens next in the classroom. Standardized test scores tell teachers very little about the students and generally create more problems with differentiated instruction and individualized planning. Also, teachers create assessments because we know they are effective tools (and we often share with other teachers and collaborate without being told to). We assess our kids for free, because we know it's right. We don't believe that paying Pearson for expensive contracts is going to help at all.

4. *Test results are used inappropriately.* When test results do come from above, we quickly find that the advertised reason for them was a lot of nonsense. The fact is, the standardized testing happening across the nation has very little to nothing to do with evaluating students, and

everything to do with evaluating teachers and schools on one—and only one, regardless of what the propaganda says—measure. One very poor and misaligned measure.

5. *Kids learn that life is a multiple-choice test.* I do realize that the two huge national testing consortia are trying to introduce "revolutionary" new types of test items into their computer-based assessments, but it means very little. I've seen examples of those super items, and they do not come even close to the types of authentic assessments that teachers and teacher leaders have been creating and sharing for years. Even if life isn't multiple choice, kids will be trained that the entire worth of their existence is based on the ability to pass one large measure of an incredibly narrow and prescribed skill base. This leaves out all of the other things that can't be standardized and tested. We know it, kids know it, and parents know it.

6. *Kids aren't learning meaningful skills and concepts.* The Common Core Standards and the high-stakes testing push aside or leave out vital parts of growing up and succeeding in school and in the world beyond. Even in the most dedicated classrooms and among the most innovative and creative teachers, students have grown accustomed to the expectations of passing a series of exams based on common standards that end up defining their performance for the entire school year. Students that are unlucky enough to have a high rate of non-

proficiency end up losing the things that make school so special for many of them: music, art, drama, social times, and the ability to step outside of the drill-and-kill zone for a little bit of much needed fun.

7. *Computer-adaptive tests are invalid.* Pearson recently joined forces with College Board to launch the all-new Accuplacer, the placement testing system used often in colleges and universities. Pearson added its online remediation program to the system to create a digital environment where students can take online tests to determine where their strengths and weaknesses are and then take online courses to try to boost those skills. Honestly, this sounds pretty neat for a student in later grades who is looking to get ahead or for students who need to catch up with certain skills. However, when the Smarter Balanced Assessment Consortium uses this system as the base model of its entire assessment program—for *all* kids—it becomes clear that this is simply a moneymaking scheme. Especially after seeing how flawed those tests tend to be. Also, the items are adaptive, and they can't possibly be used to assess all students, across common standards, to be used for teacher evaluation or other high-stakes purposes.

8. *Kids are suffering physical and mental distress.* It's incredible how little I actually knew about the real scale of how badly these tests and the surrounding culture were hurting kids when I published *Children of the Core.*

I included some personal stories and I knew of some pretty severe cases, but the scale of this problem is much larger than we know—much larger than we're allowed to know.

The two national testing consortia (PARCC and SBAC) are designed to be standardized not only the testing across the country, but also to begin the work of standardizing the actual curriculum that is being aligned to the Common Core. We are seeing already how states are contracting companies to create standard curricular modules for grade level English-language arts and mathematics, with the intent of making sure teachers are teaching what they're supposed to, in preparation for the standardized tests, on which their evaluations are to be based. As I've mentioned before, the days when a teacher can close the door and teach as she wants to are quickly waning, and it has already been reported that teachers are being reprimanded for not sticking to the plan.[73]

Also, the new Smarter Balanced (SBAC) computer-based assessments have obviously been modeled on the Oregon OAKS platform; looking at the new Smarter Balanced practice items, and comparing them to the OAKS format, confirms this idea.[74] It's not shocking or unprecedented that SBAC copies OAKS, since Oregon is a governing member, it just seems to be a cheap method to "redesign" this apparently revolutionary testing system. Although, I'm sure that Oregon has been the experiment for quite some time.

What is shocking, or at least disturbing, is what SBAC thinks a *performance assessment* should look like. If the practice test available online is any indication, the performance that SBAC is trying to measure is simply using "evidence" from text selections to form short answers.[75]

More and more students complain that school has become nothing but a long, scripted series of worksheets and "units" that don't interest them and don't allow them to ask too many questions or think on their own. This is especially true of middle and high school kids, who start to really feel the need to have their voices heard and their opinions valued (if those desires haven't already been "schooled" out of them). This new set of programmatic learning modules attempts to silence the student voice and keep them in neat little lines to follow the program.

State Longitudinal Data Systems

Statewide data systems in public schools are certainly not new. Every state has one, which keeps student data for grades, test scores, immunization records, address history, discipline and behavior history, and more. These have proven to be beneficial for kids who move from one school to another or between districts, especially in areas with high mobility. They have also been protected under the Family Educational Rights and Protection Act of 1974 (FERPA), which states clearly that the school systems that collect and store data on students may not share educational records or data with any other entities (other than those deemed necessary to provide needed services or who otherwise need access for the best interests of the child) unless parental permission is granted.

FERPA was probably already a little too loose on the whole sharing part, but Arne Duncan didn't think so. In 2013, the Department of Education changed the privacy regulations of FERPA to allow easier sharing and access by third-party and private entities, including those that are data mining for the purpose of selling education materials to targeted groups and individuals. In other words, the Department of Education just opened up vast databases of student data (including personally identifiable data) to private corporations looking for direct sales. This move was done with no Congressional knowledge or action, since it a department-level action, and with President Obama's approval.

The most obvious type of data that these corporations want and need are test scores—the all-important product that also acts as currency in the "market-based" education system. Using student test scores and aggregate data from schools, private textbook and testing corporations know exactly where to send their representatives to sell intervention and remediation materials. But that's not all. This type of data also alerts privatization reformers and charter management corporations which districts need to be circled, bid on, and ultimately bought by inserting Broad- or Friedman- or Walton-supported leadership (see Denver, Chicago, Philadelphia, New York City, Douglas County, CO, and Syracuse, for a few examples).

Finally, it serves as a convenient database of future members of the American workforce as they move up through the grades, which collects everything that a future employer could possibly want to know about a high school graduate. Here is a tiny sample of the 400-plus data points being collected by companies like inBloom and other state database systems:

1. Students name and parent name(s)
2. PSID (no Social Security number needed)
3. Address and address history
4. Student bus stop location and bus number
5. Student free or reduced lunch status
6. Previous report cards and test scores
7. School-level health records*
8. Disciplinary and behavioral records
9. Attendance records
10. Parent educational attainment
11. Parent criminal records
12. Parent work and income history

As I mentioned, much of this data has very little, if anything, to do with helping a child learn, engage, or improve. Some of it is data that has been collected and stored by school systems for a long time, but is now being centralized and, again, made available for those parties that have an educational interest. Unfortunately, that term is very vague and can be interpreted in many different ways.[76]

Finally, the Gates Foundation's investments into biometric data collection is destined to be added to this list, giving an added measure of student engagement and interest throughout their school careers, which will be used to evaluate teaching practice (not curriculum) and will no doubt be added to the longitudinal data for workforce "readiness." In other words, if a student is bored, lazy, or otherwise disengaged, it may affect career prospects in the future.

In Summary

The entire education reform movement has two strong goals that billionaires, millionaires, and corporations have invested into, and for which politicians have voraciously supported through legislation and policy.

1. Take advantage of the next big profit venture in America. They tanked the housing and mutual fund market, so they need a new target. Rupert Murdoch reminded us of the $500 billion dollar industry that is public education, and why we should get a piece of the action.

2. Turn public schools into private workforce training centers, which will feed into a flooding labor market and drive down wages and the need for expensive benefits and pensions. Oh, and while we're at it, we'll completely destroy the unions.

I don't like the Common Core Standards because they're poorly written, not backed up by academic research, ignore solid cognitive and developmental research, and are the foundation of a national testing and data collection monstrosity set up by Race to the Top. But, they're *not* the only means to the end of corporate takeover of America's public schools. I will write more about that in the last chapter.

My state of New York just released test scores from the grades 3-8 Common Core aligned tests on Wednesday, August 7. We were warned for months, even before we had any idea what the tests would look like, that we would probably see a significant drop in scores—up to 30% lower. This is a setup, and it's not rocket science to figure it out. As Stephen Krashen told me recently, "Test scores are always low when a new test is introduced. Then they get better as students and teachers get more familiar with the test." Education Commissioner John King knows that; everyone knows that. But this is just the beginning.

This year, according to a memo he sent to superintendents a few days prior, he wants leaders to use the scores "judiciously" when making staffing decisions.[77] That doesn't sound good in its vagueness. "Judicious" means "with good judgment or good sense." Considering the mandates and initiatives King has put in place in the past couple of years, if he is the example of "judicious" decision-making, we're all in trouble.

The American Federation of Teachers (AFT) and the New York State Union of Teachers (NYSUT) called on the New York State Education Department (NYSED) to hold off on using state test results in teacher performance evaluation (APPR), until those teachers are given a chance to get a better curriculum in their hands. John King answered in two ways:

1. By saying "No."
2. By contracting, last year, (at a cost of $12.9 million) Core Knowledge Foundation, Expeditionary Learning, and Common Core, Inc., to write curriculum modules so that

teachers don't have to make lessons anymore.[78] They just have to follow the script if they want to get good scores out of their students and save their jobs.

King calls these first CCSS test results the new benchmarks for future achievement measures. If you knew how disastrous these April tests were in New York, you would agree with me when I say that there is no validity to their results. Using invalid test scores as benchmarks is not only stupid, it's also strongly unethical.

What New York teachers and parents should be angry about is the fact that King doesn't care about the validity of any of this. He wants to sell real estate. He is ready to sell us out. He wants teachers out of the way. This is one way to accomplish that. In light of the goings-on in North Carolina, recently, it should be pretty obvious at this point that politicians and education chiefs will stop at nothing to follow through with the plans that their corporate reform puppetmasters have mandated, like the ones I discussed in chapter two. And what New York's state chief is trying to accomplish is being parroted by state chiefs nationwide—including your state.

What I'm truly opposed to are the many moves taken by so-called "philanthropists" to rebuild our school system using methods and legislation that are not only based on lies, but that simply can't work in the best interest of our kids. We know that's not the goal, however, so it's up to us—the parents, teachers, citizens, civic groups, and students. We have to be our children's protectors from this corporate assault on their futures.

I have collected several stories from around the nation about people who have found their voices and their passions, and who have chosen to stand up against terrifying power and wealth for the sake of our children and our country's future. The following pages do not represent even close to a true image of the massive protests, actions, and activism I've seen, but it does provide a start. I want to showcase some people and groups that I believe have done brave and important things, and I want to hold them up as models for those who wish to join the fight.

I hope you enjoy and are motivated by these tales of the effects and the responses to what's happening to our schools. I have not changed any names (only omitted a few), as those who offered me their stories wanted to make it known that they are proud to stand up for their own rights and the rights of children.

The Baby and the Bathwater

PART TWO

Grassroots

I will be as harsh as truth, and uncompromising as justice... I am in earnest, I will not equivocate, I will not excuse, I will not retreat a single inch, and I will be heard.

William Lloyd Garrison

CHAPTER

4

Mama Bears, Tea Parties, and Occupy Education

Parent Activists

Out of the ashes of the revolutionary opt-out movement in New York State, and elsewhere, rose several groups of very strong-willed moms (and, yes, dads) that knew simply refusing an end-of-the-year test wasn't enough to effect lasting changes. After all, the tests were causing anxiety and distress, but that wasn't where the real problems were coming from. After only a few weeks, the Long Island Opt-Out group on Facebook had grown to over 8,000 new members, most of who were moms and dads wanting to know how to fight the overwhelming testing culture that had invaded and taken over their schools. They educated themselves about the inner workings of the New York State Education Department, they called the commissioner's office asking questions, they organized, and they chose to boycott the end of the year state tests in April. The introduction goes into why so many made the choice, but boycotting wasn't enough.

More and more information poured in to the social groups and more and more outrage boiled toward the surface. Long Island parents engaged the media to get their stories told, showed up to board of education meetings to voice their opposition to the changes they saw, and started to organize into more focused groups, aimed at the various other issues in education. Some groups continued to target the unfair testing practices, some focused on corporate influences on the school boards, and others began to question and investigate the Common Core and other national mandates.

Two highly motivated mama bears made a splash in Long Island, even after the test revolt had begun to settle and the dust was clearing. In April 2013, Jeanine Baxter-Cozzetti formed the single-issue action group, Parents and Teachers Against Common Core (P-TACC), which caught on very quickly with fellow parents from the Tri-state area and grew to a couple thousands members virtually overnight. According to the group's mission, Cozzetti was looking to organize people and affect the state leadership in order to pull New York State out of Race to the Top and the Common Core Standards.

Soon, Cozzetti found another strong and determined parent and school employee, Sara Wottawa, who spend hours upon hours researching the ins and outs of the Federal education changes and connections with the states and various corporations. (Wottawa was also active in the United Opt Out movement.) With Cozzetti's publicity and marketing prowess and Wottawa's incredible knack for finding relatively well-hidden information, they became a force with which to be reckoned.

P-TACC's goals were to restore the state's Constitutional right, via the 10th Amendment, to control education locally; to draft a bill to withdraw New York State from the Common Core; and to release New York from the Federal Race to the Top program requirements of (1) common standards, (2) teachers evaluations linked to state test scores, and (3) data collections system used to track, access, and share student information.

The group quickly put a petition in place, which gathered several hundred signatures relatively quickly, which was to be sent to Governor Cuomo and state legislators. They also drafted their own model bill, based on those of Georgia and Indiana, and dedicated plenty of time calling and educating policymakers around the state. Finally, they began a successful education campaign in several areas of the Island to bring awareness to parents, teachers, and citizens about what was happening to Long Island's schools.

I was lucky enough to be contacted by Mrs. Cozzetti to help spread the word and speak to audiences, as well as take part in conference calls, which she shared online to further the cause. She recruited passionate, lively, and highly informative speakers to engage the audiences and get Long Island residents to sign the petition, make phone calls during "blitzes," and picket local lawmakers' offices.

On July 18, 2013, P-TACC held a press conference with New York Assemblyman Al Graf to announce the drafting of New York State Assembly Bill A07994 – an act to amend the education law, in relation to the Common Core State Standards Initiative and the Race to the Top Program. P-TACC organized more phone blitzes to statewide representatives to garner support for the bill. As of the writing of this book, it remains to be seen where this will go. I encourage my readers to follow P-TACC on their website.

Just prior to the actions of P-TACC, two Indiana moms made national waves by taking similar actions. A year earlier, Indiana governor, Mitch Daniels, promoted the Common Core Standards, alongside the hardline state superintendent, Tony Bennett, who has broken ethics codes and laws to support privatization schemes. It appeared that the standards were there to stay. Heather Crossin and Erin Tuttle were the moms that brought it down, at least for now.

Crossin and Tuttle saw research and talked to experts that suggested the CCSS were actually reducing the levels of knowledge, skills, and expectations in Indiana schools. The pair questioned the leadership relentlessly and only received answers that were not adequate to defend the standards which had taken over the schools. What seemed to be the last straw for them was the state's lean toward a "voucher" system of school choice, which relied on religious schools agreeing to adopt new state tests aligned to the CCSS. Being parents of Catholic school students, Crossin and Tuttle found that to be completely unacceptable.

With the help of several state and national groups, the duo made it a mission to educate the leadership of the state, which didn't seem to have a clue what was happening or what all of this really was (a problem in almost every state's legislature). After a failed first attempt to get a bill passed to drop Common Core, the moms, with the help of Senator Schneider, drew up a new bill and rallied the state parents and teachers to support its passing.

During the rallying, the incumbent superintendent was replaced by a Glenda Ritz, who had expressed concern about the state's adoption of the Common Core. The election resulted in a very serious landfall and a changing of the guard. The bill to withdraw Indiana from the Common Core passed, causing outrage among corporate supporters, and started a wave that has been spreading ever since. Several other states (such as New York, above) have introduced legislation to suspend, withdraw, or change Common Core and Race to the Top initiatives, and many state leaders are asking for better understanding from the Federal government about the realities of the mandates on to which their state education departments have signed.

Sometimes, very small groups of people can make very large changes.

One of the more well-known groups of moms comes from Utah and continues to update their website, "Education Without Representation," and has been speaking around the country about Common Core and the other ills of education reform.[79] Christel

Swasey, Renee Braddy, and Alisa Ellis have taken their message against education reform to the state board of education meetings, the local board meetings, and across the country, in support of "high quality, real education and local control," which is a message I can support. Swasey tells a story not unlike mine: she was a teacher of high school English until she found she could not support the curriculum embedded in and supported by the Common Core.

The website that Swasey maintains, along with her other two cohorts, is kept up regularly with the intent of educating all who read it about Common Core, privacy issues around data collection, and the rapid decline in literature instruction in public schools. She also voices her statements against the growing tendency of states and districts to use kids as guinea pigs in several different trials and initiatives, without parental consent. This is also a concern I share. There's no excuse for drug testing, surveying, testing, or experimenting on children without advance, express permission from parents and guardians. Yet, it seems to happen almost every week.

These moms have laid plenty of groundwork for others to follow, and follow they do. In many states, I have read moms and dads organize to create larger spheres of influence and education based on the work that Swasey, Braddy, and Ellis have done and which they share freely. This is how a movement gains momentum, with education and tireless dedication to the cause.

These mom and dad groups are meant to be replicated. Parents, as we have said over and over, are the keys to ending this corporate and Federal takeover of our schools and putting the whole system back into the hands of the real stakeholders, instead of just the shareholders. Their lesson: find more moms and dads and ask the question, "How's school going for your kids? What changes have you noticed? Let's get some people together and talk about it."

Moms and dads have been successful spreading the word by hosting house parties, organizing large meetups at school board meetings, handing out flyers in their communities, and starting letter-writing campaigns. Obviously, stay-at-home moms have seen more success, since they can allocate the time to write letters to the editors of newspapers and elected officials. But even single parents and homes in which both parents work can launch successful education campaigns. Busy parents have told me that they found great success invading stagnant PTAs and getting them mobilized. Just because the National PTA has bought into this whole mess doesn't mean that local PTAs have; if the local group has already had too much Common Core Kool-aid to drink, then strongly consider starting a new PTO. Even meeting up on weekends for barbecues in the neighborhood parks and asking for booth space at county fairs and similar events have worked out well for many.

The point is, parents need to talk and start asking more questions. Then, they need to begin to figure out ways to start taking targeted action. Every community is different, and many different strategies may need to be tried before some reaction is seen. Pressure those legislators, ladies and gentlemen. You'd be surprised how many of them really just don't know what's going on. I believe that this year, or perhaps the next year, when things get really messy and confusing and harmful, we will see the fire light up under a critical mass of angry parents. Start now. Get people to open their eyes and look around the world surrounding their kids. This can't wait. It has to start now!

See the Appendix for great resources and tools to help find a state group or organization to help get started.

Tea Parties, 9-12 Groups, and Libertarians

I'll be honest: I had no idea what to expect when giving my first presentations to Tea Party and 9-12 Patriot groups during my first circuit. I'm one of those people who never ventured to meet people who collectively fight large and invasive issues with conviction and organization. I've never shown to up to a large, real-life Occupy protest (that's next) and I never showed up to a Tea Party meeting or protest. So, I allowed my predeterminations, which were created from what I saw in the media, guide me into these meetings. And, admittedly, I was a little nervous.

I was also totally wrong. And so is the media. I could tell that some of the people who invited me to speak were a little unsure of me, as well. It's been printed more than once that I lean politically to the left, so it had to have felt a little risky for them, wondering if I would say something that might upset their membership. The fact is, there are still some differences in how we interpret this education takeover and I hope that I was able to make a small contribution to the movement they have been building.

I'll be blunt, as I was in the beginning of the book. Tea Party icons are not entirely correct or informed about what's really happening. I agree with much of what Glenn Beck and others have been saying, but there's also some misunderstanding. Beck often talks about the dangers of communism, Nazism, and the New World Order. These points are somewhat stretchy for me, however, since I can see that there is no communist idea at play here and there are too many definitions of the New World Order to actually pin it down to a real argument. If what they are referring to is Agenda 21, then I've already touched on that. The United States has too much pride and corporate power to just start loving everyone and giving up sovereignty.

Will this blur national borders? Certainly. Billionaires and corporations don't have patriotic feelings or national pride. They have power and wealth. That's about all. It should certainly worry the Tea Party movement that corporate power is currently undermining American education, since it effectively training students with the mindset that they need to play for the "right" team. Not the American team, by the way. Children are indeed being targeted to start thinking less nationalistically and more with an allegiance to the employers with which they will soon match up. Honestly, this worries me too.

During my presentations, I've heard questions about socialism and fascism and communism, and I've answered with realistic nightmares of corporatism and privatization. Every single time, I've had people come up to me after the presentation and thank me. This is actually scarier than anything they'd heard before. The corporatization of our kids and our country, it appears, is worse than becoming socialist.

By their own admission, Tea Party groups are notoriously spread out and difficult to organize. They tend to remain locally active, only coming together to join large protests, like the few in Washington, D.C. that we've seen recently. It's nice to know that such scattered groups can be called to action so quickly, but they've also started to realize that the groups must remain closely connected for this issue. A good example is happening in Pennsylvania, which is a large state with several groups in many different localities. However, under the main title, Pennsylvanians Against the Common Core, a large, statewide network has grown that unites them (and others) and puts them in constant contact.

This has worked well, since it shows a larger group in solidarity against the policies that are pushing Common Core and increased testing throughout the state. Pennsylvania has a relatively weak governor and a schools chief planted by Jeb Bush's FEE organization to enact laws and mandates for the privatization of public schools. That governor is also quite constantly put in his place by large corporate interests, like ExxonMobil, which likes to remind the governor of the money they've invested in schools and industry. Much the way the mafia would remind a small business of the protection they've provided over the years; not yet extortion, but certainly coercion.

In any case, the Tea Party groups in Pennsylvania have played a large part in the back-and-forth game of politics in that state. When the governor makes an unpopular move, the Tea Party rises to the response. At one point, the governor tried to put the brakes on the Common Core implementation requirements across the state, in part due to the activism of the Tea Party. That's when ExxonMobil came back with the letter and the suggestion to the governor to get back on track.

I don't want to sound patronizing, but I believe the Tea Party would be a force to deal with if it became more focused, more firm, and more educated on the realities of the current education reform movement. Trying to link Race to the Top and all of its pieces to things like the UN New World Order, Agenda 21, communism, or other national threats make it too easy for the left and the media to ridicule them. I'm not completely discounting their theories, since I've seen reasons to be concerned, but there simply isn't enough evidence to start sounding loud alarm bells in those directions quite yet. There are more destructive forces at work in this country with more domestic agendas.

The evidence to date points to two large groups (the super-rich and the government) with basically the same goal: to train our children to become obedient workers in an American economy that intends to remain dominant in the world. The Tea Party needs to start setting its sights on the corporate powers that are running the government, as well as the politicians that are being hired to make it legal for them to do so. The Tea Party is most concerned with their individual liberties, which means that it's in their best interest to start understanding that the rise of mega-corporations is a direct threat to that liberty.

I will make one suggestion here though, since I know that UN intervention is one of the things the Tea Party and other libertarian groups are worried about. The fact that Rahm Emanuel has shown such disregard for poor kids in Chicago, has closed badly needed schools, and has shown no apparent remorse about it raises my eyebrows. The fact that he already knew that closing schools in poor and dangerous neighborhoods would increase crime and hunger rates—and it has already started to happen epidemically in those communities—makes me wonder what his problem is, and those who work for him and have gladly carried out his dirty work.

And then, after a relatively short time, the United Nations said that Chicago should be investigated as a potential human rights violation due to the treatment of poor, minority students. That does make me think a little more broadly. President Obama and Arne Duncan have said little about the Chicago closings, and have done even less about them. Rahm Emanuel has close ties to the president and the secretary. Just let your guard down for a little bit. Did the president expect this? If so, why? Was this just one way to invite the global police force into our borders? Is that a good thing? Or does the Chicago Club not care because there's nothing too threatening about the UN? There are still so many questions.

The point is, just because the protests are coming from a group that the politicians and the media like to label "fringe," doesn't mean that we should close our eyes to the possibilities of which they speak. I've spent many days hearing claims and arguments and questions from many different groups. I've not discounted a single one, but instead sought the answers and the most likely truth. I have no evidence of the strong connection between Agenda 21 and the Common Core Standards; in fact, I see a very big disconnect between the corporate agenda of winner-takes-all and the UN agenda of everyone-save-the-planet. That doesn't necessarily mean I'm right. I, like every other concerned citizen, am constantly seeing and learning new things. We have to stop the prejudices against the petty things we don't like about each other and start understanding and educating each other.

Which brings me to another "fringe" group.

Occupy Education

When the Occupy Wall Street movement started camping out in protest in New York City, it was unprecedented. It certainly got our attention, if nothing else. And it certainly got the attention of the Wall Street bankers, corporations, and media moguls, who wasted no time at all launching a large smear campaign against them. At the same time I heard bankers and pundits call them homeless, dirty, undisciplined, and a group of animals, I saw documents come out of the Occupy movement that were written with great intelligence, sober thinking, and a real mind toward improvement of the economic future of America. Obviously, those documents and statements were never allowed to be seen by the mainstream, and we continued on making fun of them.

The Occupy movement suffers the same logistical barrier as the Tea Party—there are too many splinter groups scattered around the country. Many of them go by different names and tend to stay isolated. Social media does tend to alleviate some of the isolation, as they share with other groups their stories, protest dates, and other actions. I have to wonder, though, if they may be gun shy about rallying up another demonstration of the scope of the original protest. Or, perhaps the energy is different. The first campout demonstration was more or less spontaneous as a reaction to the economic downturn and outrageous effects, such as foreclosures, job loss, and the spike in the poverty level—things which average Americans also sympathized with. Education is different. Most Americans, I would venture to guess, have neither a clear idea of the things I've discussed in this book, nor how it all affects them. Would another large-scale Occupy action, dedicated to education, allow the media another chance to make them look bad? Would that effectively ostracize that movement from the society at large?

So, we see smaller actions. In April of 2013, I joined a relatively small group of activists from around the country to protest the destructive policies coming out of the U.S. Department of Education building in Washington, D.C. The event was organized by the tireless United Opt Out group, which has been a pioneering force in fighting high-stakes testing policies and other reform agendas. The event was title Occupy the D.O.E. in 2012, so it only made sense to call this next year's event Occupy the D.O.E. 2.0.

There was no mainstream media smear campaign. No pundits called us unruly, smelly bums. In fact, there was almost no media coverage at all, other than a few radio stations and several blogs. For the record, no one slept outside the building. We all stayed in hotels or with relatives. We were all teachers, parents, and students who wanted to stand in front of the building responsible for harmful policies and make our voices heard. We were not of the same political party and we spanned the left-right spectrum. We were there for our kids, their schools, and their teachers.

As scattered as they are, all Occupy groups seem to agree with the following position statement from a Nebraska Occupy Education group:

> *Nobody should be denied education because of their socioeconomic status; nobody should be forced into overwhelming debt for a degree. As curious and creative creatures, education is something that should be a basic part of who we are for our entire lives. Education should not merely be a necessary step that we take to get a career. It should be something we engage in everyday, for the sheer joy of learning, and for the betterment of ourselves and our community.*

I have not read or seen any position statements regarding education from the Tea Party or other libertarians, but I have heard individual members echo the above quite strongly. Education should be available to all kids, all citizens, *and should be free national government or corporate control.*

I put that last part in italics because it's a relatively new agreement between the right and the left. Historically, the left

181

wing has been distrustful of corporations and their role in society; the right wing has been distrustful of the Federal government and its role in society (particularly the size of that government). This time, you're starting to see a convergence in thought—neither side trusts any of them anymore. Perhaps that's as it should be. During this period of time when we've been focused on distrusting each other, the corporate-government moves to grab more power and wealth have gone unchecked by either side. Our vigilance needs to return to where it matters.

Coming Together

In July 2013, a small, unlikely group launched a website called the Left-Right Alliance for Education to meet the unholy alliance of corporate and government power. This group was created to maintain a multi-partisan position against the Common Core State Standards Initiative (CCSSI), as well as the testing and privacy problems that come with it. This group includes contributors that nearly represent all parts of the current political and ideological makeup in equal parts. The members of this alliance welcome endorsements from others who agree the main mission and idea behind the group's creation:

> We oppose the CCSSI because it continues the failed education reforms of the past and violates privacy rights as it builds a system for centrally managed student training for the future workforce of the "Global Economy." This central goal will dismantle liberal arts education, which most contributes to the development of mature

thinkers who are prepared to thrive in any chosen life path and sustain a free civilization.

The message I get is that both left and right leaning parents want to see their children offered an education that prepares them for life and everything that come with it, not just the workforce.

While the Common Core Standards are the main target for many activist and information groups (P-TACC, Parents and Educators Against the Common Core, Stop Common Core groups in multiple states), they aren't the only civic grassroots efforts trying to save education. Parents have also grown the anti-testing movement across the country, which I mentioned at the beginning of the book. Additionally, the privacy concerns of the statewide data collection systems are concerning enough to start widespread petitions and even lawsuits.

I believe that the corporate reforms were planned out with the idea that once the unions and teachers were under the power elite's thumb, the going would be easy from there. I don't think they expected the uprising and resistance from the parents or the communities that we've seen lately. The word keeps spreading and the movement to end this attack on schools is becoming more organized and locally focused.

There is still one depressingly underrepresented group of people in this fight, however: those living in poverty and who are seeing the most devastating effects of education reform in their very neighborhoods. Of course, teachers who teach in high-poverty areas will stand behind them and fight for them, but the lack of conversation about poverty and its effects seems out of proportion with the importance of tackling that problem. Parents who live in poverty feel pressured to stay quiet and work hard in order to simply stay afloat, but they also feel powerless to change their plight and fight against a system that targets them first. Becoming active means fighting for and alongside all parents, regardless of ZIP code or background. If we choose to use our voices, it will be for all children, everywhere.

We've been saying it since the beginning of the opt-out movement: *parents are the key to change.* If you are a parent, and you know other parents, realize that you have the true power in your hands to make things happen for the good of your kids. We have numbers, votes, voices, and a strong desire to protect our kids from these snakes in the grass. Join an organization in your state. Find a Facebook group that opposes Common Core, high-stakes testing, or other reform and engage in the discussions and actions. (And remember to stay away from Parent Revolution.)

CHAPTER

5

The Locals, Dropouts, and BATs

This chapter is about the teacher movement, which has been relatively quiet, until recently, and for good reason. The idea of speaking out against the things that are changing classrooms in such negative ways has been equated with disciplinary actions, threats of job loss, and slander from leadership and the media. Therefore, most teachers thought it better to play it safe, ignore the outside, and do what they're supposed to do: teach their students. Several parent and political groups have asked me during my presentations, "where are the teachers in all of this?" and, "where are their unions?" I tell them that the teachers are upset and feeling the pressure from within to speak up, take action, and make a change; they're also under immense pressure to keep quiet, toe the line, and do as they're told.

Earlier this year, in Seattle, Washington, a group of teachers at Garfield High School organized as a staff and simply refused to administer the Measures of Academic Progress (MAP) test that is mandated by the district. The teachers stated that the test did not show student academic progress, unfairly rated teachers' practice, wasted precious instructional days and resources, and was an expense that the district could not afford. The teacher boycott made national headlines and brought together students and parents to support those teachers. A few days after the Garfield boycott, another area high school, Ballard, followed suit. Ultimately, three more high schools would join the boycott. Teachers and students held their collective breath to see what consequences would fall onto the brave faculties.

What was pleasantly surprising—even shocking—was that the teachers ultimately won. After some threatening talk from the Washington State Education Department, State Superintendent finally declared the MAP testing as optional.[80]

New York State has been a hotbed of controversy and action this past school year. Almost immediately following the Seattle boycotts, a small western New York district in Hamburg faced a choice: either submit a teacher evaluation system based on student growth (i.e. test scores) that is acceptable to the Education Commissioner, or face sanctions, including loss of state funding. Governor Andrew Cuomo had required local districts and teachers unions to agree on and submit those Annual Professional Performance Review (APPR) plans, while dangling a carrot worth couple hundred thousand dollars in funding as the collateral.

Hamburg teachers refused to make standardized test scores a major part of their APPR, thus allowing the superintendent unreasonable power to fire teachers, which left the Hamburg district and local union at a stalemate.

Unfortunately, three months after the plan's due date, the Hamburg teachers were left in the dark as their union president struck a deal with the district. Although the district denied it, many teachers reported being threatened with job loss if they did not comply. Also, the state Education Commissioner stated that he would step in and impose a plan if one could not be agreed upon. And anyone who knows anything about New York's Education Commissioner knows that the results would not have been pretty.

Also in New York State, during the parent opt-out uprising this spring, several teachers reportedly had parents asking for advice about how to opt out and what would happen if they did. Several teachers who supported these parents and students in their choice obliged, offering to try to smooth the way for the students to refuse and to try and make the action as cordial as possible. Obviously, teachers still have to administer the test, according to the state law, but many wanted to find ways to move the boycotters to separate locations to read, do alternative assignments, or at least be away from the testing room.

These types of benign actions landed many teachers in positions to face administrative actions and severe warnings. Teachers reported being reprimanded and "coached" by school and district leaders, suspended for various amounts of time, and told to stay quiet about the state tests or face the possibility of breaking state security rules (which is totally odd and reeks of fear mongering). When a teacher breaks test security protocol, he or she risks loss of a teaching license. Several teachers were pointedly reminded of this (many were threatened) and told not to speak to parents at all about opting out of the tests.

Unsupported, unheard, and constantly under the gun, teachers have been looking for ways to speak up, take action, and be a part of the change they knew needs to happen. The problem is, most of them believe, rightly so, that their jobs are at stake if they break their silence. They need numbers and they need a united voice. One question from several different sources has been, "Where are the teachers unions?" Some teachers who felt those threats personally turned to their local union representatives, who then turned to the state union leadership for guidance and, hopefully, protection.

What they received instead qualifies as neither.

The state teachers union, New York State Union of Teachers (NYSUT) instead sent out a statewide memo making sure that teachers were aware that assisting parents and students in their decisions to opt out could result in consequences, including termination. NYSUT also discouraged teachers from taking part in any type of activism or even answering questions about the tests. There were no provisions of what actions they should take and there was no sense, whatsoever, that NYSUT would have their back if they did decide to exercise their First Amendment rights as American citizens. Let me make it clear, also, that the hundreds of teachers I heard from during that time stated that they only talked about the tests when they were out of the school building and not on paid time. It seemed that the unions had left teachers to fend for themselves, with only the advice of keeping quiet. But then, after it was all said and done, NYSUT came to the rescue!

On June 8, 2013, NYSUT held a large rally to bring teachers and others to Albany, New York, to show the state educational leadership how we felt about the way things were going. It was widely publicized and very well-funded. Big names were scheduled to speak, including the president of the American Federation of Teachers, Randi Weingarten. Buses were chartered across the state to get as many teachers as possible to join the rally and the mall of the Empire State Plaza in Albany, New York, was set up like a rock concert. NYSUT was ready to make some noise!

If you've ever wondered where you can find the biggest collection of superheroes, find a place where there are lots and lots of public school teachers. Find a place that looked like Albany's Empire State Plaza on June 8, 2013. This is the day when almost 20,000 educators, parents, and citizens showed up to tell the New York State Education Department that it's time to kick politics and corporations out of our schools and let teachers and administrators do what they're meant to do: teach children to be ready for life. Not "college" and not "career." Life.

It wasn't entirely clear that the message from the union leadership was the same. NYSUT president Dick Iannuzzi kept saying, "Get it right," and AFT president Randi Weingarten kept saying, "Put the brakes on the stakes."

The energy was decidedly electric, and it was clear why all of those people were standing in the crowd. They were there for the freedom to teach the kids they care about in the best ways they know are possible. They all agreed on one important fact: high-stakes testing is the absolute worst way to teach and evaluate and, for kids, the absolute worst way to learn.

But, there was a quality to this rally that made the more cynical among us pay closer attention. The *One Voice United* rally was just that: a *rally* to get everyone on the same page in the push to end New York's high-stakes testing regime that has plagued our schools and our students for long enough. This year was especially tough on kids, since the tests were aligned to the Common Core State Standards, which were not fully implemented and for which teachers and students were not prepared. So, NYSUT and AFT attempted to create "One Voice" to slow it all down.

Randi Weingarten is not shy about her support of the Common Core Standards, even as it is an untested and overbearing system that is inappropriate at the early elementary levels and overly restrictive at the secondary levels. In fact, she was the only speaker at the rally to even mention Common Core–and she yelled (very loudly) her support. I have to wonder why she was there to begin with. The local speakers (superintendents, teachers, other New Yorkers) were doing just fine. It was almost as if she had to have her voice included as part of the One Voice to make sure that Common Core was included.

Which brings me to the "One Voice" part. As I walked through the crowd, I realized that there were many different voices, asking for many different issues to be considered. Some wanted to restore arts, some wanted to get rid of corporate influence, some wanted to get rid of the Common Core, and many wanted local control restored.

Randi's message was none of those; or, worse, a contradiction of those. She said we can restore arts and music alongside the Common Core. Perhaps. But we cannot restore local control with Common Core. That would be a contradiction. Common Core is one of the requirements of a Federal mandate put in place to remove local control. Dick Iannuzzi stands alongside Randi in this regard, although he doesn't seem to have the guts to say it out loud (other than to chant, "get it right!" over and over). Both of them were instrumental in helping to push through the punishing annual professional performance reviews (APPR) that have teachers biting their nails. Both of them have proven that their ideas and cooperation with state officials are harmful.

The point is, I hope that the rally on the mall got one thing started: the realization that local unions–not the state or national unions–are the harbingers of change here. There are plenty in this state and this nation that know what's best for their own communities. If this realization comes to head, it may be the change we need. After all, local control is what we need to bring public education back to its pre-NCLB flexibility to raise creative thinkers and innovators, as we tear down the cronyism and corporatism of Race to the Top.

The rally accomplished two things:

1. (Hopeful and encouraging) It made teachers realize that they are not alone. The state of New York has a very large group of teachers who feel the same ways, see the same things, and all want change. This is empowering. This will hopefully get teachers to move and get active

with their *local* union chapters and start organizing in order to return the profession to the way it should be. Teachers are powerful and they have parents on their side. This is for our kids and we should refuse to accept anything but what we know is best for them.

2. (Dangerous and orchestrated) It made AFT and NYSUT look like the helpful big brothers, as they pretend to stand up to the state and national powers that have put these policies and mandates into place. Unfortunately, AFT and NYSUT are, at best, powerless and, at worst, in cahoots with corporate reformers. This is evidenced by their hands in creating APPR models that are hurting teachers, putting schools at risk, and inviting privatization and profit schemes into our communities (which have no interest in helping kids).

When Weingarten and Iannuzzi know that the overwhelming testing program, PARCC, is coming to New York schools in 2014, it would be highly disingenuous of them both to suggest that high-stakes testing is bad. So, it's a good thing that they don't say that, and simply suggest that we should wait a little while. We don't like liars.

Weingarten and Iannuzzi are fully on board with the use of the Common Core State Standards, high-stakes testing (and a flood of other tests under PARCC), and statewide longitudinal data systems to evaluate teachers and track students. And, even if they're aren't fully and personally on board, they have been pressured to be careful and strategic about what they say. They do not want what so many brave and passionate teachers had written on the signs that floated above the crowd, which were mostly ignored not only by the state, but by the state and national union leaders as well. They have been given their scripts and their plans. Just like many others that we know.

In order for teachers to get back to doing what they do best, we need to get our schools back into the hands of the professionals that know how to run them. Principals and teachers, working alongside communities, parents, and post-secondary schools. Politicians, corporations, and financial advisors do not know how to run schools. It's time to put the pressure on state education departments as well, using such newfound passion and with new friends from around the state, to get us back on track. And it's way past time that teacher union leadership stops pandering to corporate interests and government takeover.

Leaving Early

Teachers are polite. Teachers want to do what's right and they want to make sure their students are safe, accounted for, and happy. They are also very trusting and always looking for the next best way to improve their own practice. These are traits that make them some of the noblest people in the world, which apparently drives greedy, soulless, and controlling elite-types crazy enough to target and scapegoat them for whatever ails the public in any given week.

Teachers are also incredibly busy. Regardless of what the media portrays, teachers are anything but lazy and underworked. They have their minds and their hearts in their jobs. Unfortunately, those same greedy "reformers" tend to use that to their advantage as they slip new mandates and initiatives into the schools and sell them as "revolutionary" and "putting students first." Finally, teachers love what they do and most will do whatever it takes to stay where they are—including extra work, even if they know it's unnecessary for their students' success.

Some teachers see it coming, feel it working its evil, and notice the harm it's doing to their kids pretty quickly. Those teachers can't stand to see it, but they also can't bring themselves to either fight it or leave it. There's fear permeating those hallowed halls of learning. A lot of fear. Sometimes, though, it reaches a breaking point.

I spent plenty of time writing about my own story in my last book, so let's look at some newer activists on the scene.

From Rhode Island, second-grade teacher, Stephen Round, left after 13 years as a revolutionary teacher. His insight in the classroom led to amazing progress in educating students with dyslexia and other difficulties that made reading challenging for them. The field of education took a serious blow when he left. I don't blame him, especially after watching him read his resignation letter on a video, which he uploaded to YouTube.[81] The video went viral over the course of a couple of weeks and stirred up more discussion about what was happening behind the walls of the school building.

Mr. Round stated that his young students were having the life and love of learning squeezed out of them by the standardized trends, and that they were increasingly forbidden to behave or think like young children. Seven-year-olds should have a healthy dose of play in their school days; Mr. Round showed that our kids were starting become more like products, locked to their desks and expected to remain on task doing menial and dry work. The kind of work that does not engage children.

Mr. Round stated that he loved working at his school and that it was a great fit. He saw success, both in his own practice and with his kids, and felt that his work with special needs students was highly gratifying, as he helped them overcome obstacles that parents thought they would just have to live with.

But then, something started to happen. According to Mr. Round, "in the attempt to confirm and abide by the misguided notions of educrats, the school system in which I had so much pride drastically changed." As new initiatives and mandates started to be implemented, Round saw a disturbing trend. "Rather than creating lifelong learners, our new goal is to create good test takers. Rather than being the recipients of a rewarding and enjoyable educational experience, our students are now relegated to experiencing a confining and demeaning education."

Like many teachers and parents, Mr. Round saw that the natural need to "be a kid" was being contained, stifled, and denied. Second graders need to socialize and be allowed to play. Play is one of those methods by which young people naturally learn to develop their speech, problem-solving, curiosity, and other life skills. It's not just a by-product of being a kid, it's a constant and powerful drive. Kids need to play and interact like they need to eat. If they don't play, they risk being stunted in their emotional and cognitive growth.

If you contain that drive and attempt to control it to the degree that Mr. Round saw in his school (and that I saw in my middle schools), you noticed that kids tend to let loose in bursts of energy, which are often deemed inappropriate. Anyone who has seen a young child cooped up in a house all day during a rainstorm knows how this ends up—kids need to explore and they need a safe place to spend those energies and in which they can exercise the drive to play. Mr. Round saw that this all-important part of schooling was being replaced by bell-to-bell teaching requirements, longer school days, and standardized test preparation. Worse, recess is used as a "bargaining chip," notes Mr. Round, and can be taken away if these little balls of pent-up energy step out of those confines.

He also mentioned something that I have thought was most disturbing. Field trips are gone. The last time I took a class on a field trip was in 2007, when I took my 6th grade science class to a museum. You know what I love about museums? The fact that you can explore and learn about all of the things that other people have collected and put on display. Whatever drives your curiosity will have a spot in a good museum. My team of teachers took our kids to a museum of natural history, which was perfect since I was teaching Earth science that year. The budgets for field trips are long gone, and we all knew that. We collected money for buses and admission from the parents, and took donations for students who couldn't afford those costs (they weren't cheap).

What really messed with me, though, is the fact that my students weren't going to be allowed to follow their curiosity and their own wonder. My team was expected to create a detailed lesson plan for the trip, including student worksheets to keep them on task. When we came back, we were expected to show evidence of student learning and to account for the fact that the trip showed "significant advancement toward achievement." To this day, I'm not quite sure what that phrase even means, but we made worksheets (with the help of the museum staff, who apparently knew about this nonsense) for the students to fill out, making sure that they stayed focused. I even had some students eagerly show me their completed worksheets and then beg to spend more time in a particular exhibit. Unfortunately, by then, we were out of time and it was time to head back to the school.

As Stephen Round wrote, "Those ventures out into the real world are...gone, gone, gone." Mr. Round continues to tutor students who need help overcome reading obstacles and he continues to develop amazing teaching methods. The last I heard from him, he was exploring a teaching opportunity at a Montessori school. I wish for him the best.

Not too long ago, I received another letter, which I helped spread around to show even more how bad this is getting. Deb Howard is another wonderful and professional teacher resigning in New York. She left on a note of sadness and respect for her colleagues. Read the letter through carefully. When we finally run the good teachers out of town, what will we have left? As we've seen over the past few years, the temp-teacher agencies and teacher bashing have led to this. And now, in addition to the mandates and threats coming from the top education brass, the union leadership has made its position clear: get on board or get out.

Identifying names have been abbreviated.

May 6, 2013

Dear Dr. M., Board of Education Members, Mrs. S.,

It is with great sadness and disappointment that I submit to you my resignation from the Brockport Central School District, effective at the close of this school year, June 30, 2013, under the provisions of our current contract.

I understand some of you may see my resignation as odd, perhaps unique, as Brockport is a wonderful school district. I feel very fortunate to have spent close to 17 years teaching here with my outstanding colleagues at Barclay School.

Yes, typically, after a long teaching career, one would announce retirement with joy and a sense of fulfillment. I am saddened, however, that I'll not be one of those individuals. I am not leaving with joy in my heart. Rather, I will leave disappointed. Disappointed in myself for being unable to finish something I started so many years ago, and disappointed with the profession I have loved since I was a little girl.

Please allow me to digress with a little background of how I was blessed to become a teacher in my Alma Mater

198

School District. Did you know "Alma Mater", a Latin phrase, actually means "Nourishing Mother"? I find it ironic that I am completing this letter the week of "Mother's Day".

Looking back, I feel much of my life's path led me to my career in Brockport. You see, I was inspired to teach by two wonderful, nourishing educators that many of you may be familiar with: Mr. G. H. and Mrs. J.B.

Mr. H. was my 6th grade teacher in 1980-81 at Barnard Elementary School in Greece. At the time, he was a young, vibrant teacher with great passion for his job and his students. He inspired me to always put forth my best effort. The "Brockport" connection is that Mr. H. is the husband of M.H., longtime beloved BCSD elementary teacher.

Shortly after moving to Brockport while in high school, Mrs. J. B. was my BHS psychology teacher. Mrs. B. was such an enthusiastic teacher who truly cared about her students. She taught a unit on child development at the time and we were able to work with young children from The Schoolhouse and present a paper on our findings. She wrote a comment to me inspiring me to continue on my path of becoming a teacher. Yes, another "nourishing mother." Ironically, Mrs. B. has been the next-door neighbor of my husband's parents for over 2 decades.

Both Mr. H. and Mrs. B. were metaphorical keys; keys that opened the door to my future career in education. Fortunately, I have had the opportunity to tell both of them that they had a positive impact on my life and my chosen career. This is what makes being a teacher so special – helping to inspire and shape lives. I am resigning because I feel as if I am no longer able to do the same for my students.

You see, over the past few years, I have seen young children filled with anxiety, not enthusiasm, over school. When I began teaching in the early 1990's, educational stress in my students was virtually non-existent. Since the mid-2000s (think No Child Left Behind/Race to the Top era) a gradual shift has been taking place in the behaviors of many children. It seems as if our youngest students, who were once eager to come to school, have been showing signs of depression, anxiety, fear, and humiliation.

Expectations are exceedingly high. The increase in "rigor" over just the past year or so, meant to get our students better prepared for "college or career" has rather placed students and teachers in a very stressful setting. Professional autonomy in the classroom is being stripped away and "modules" are taking its place.

I believe our nation is taking a dangerous path away from free, productive, creative public education and using irresponsible high-stakes testing as a means to get there. Instruction is turning into test prep and authentic learning is taking a back seat because of it. Morale is low, stress levels are high, and everyone is suffering because of it. From children to teachers to administrators all across our community, our state, and our nation, we are suffering.

My career is no longer in sync with my values. For a rather poor analogy, I liken it to a movie I saw a couple of years ago—a movie my husband and I thought was supposed to be a light-hearted comedy. Turns out, partway through, the movie was pure blasphemy. My gut told me to get up and leave the theater; this was not where we needed to be. Our values are different from what we are viewing and listening to. This is how I am feeling about the current state of education "reform." I feel I am doing a disservice to my students by subjecting them to unnecessary stress and anxiety via these soon-to-be nationalized, high-stakes standardized tests.

I'll end with a quote from Matt McElligot, children's author from the Albany area who visited our second and third graders in Barclay School this year (and in years past). He recently (May 5, 2013) had a letter published in the Times Union of Albany stating his position of our nation's craze with standardized testing.

McElligot writes, "Standardized tests measure how well students do with a narrow set of skills at one specific moment in time. To use standardized testing as the primary metric for measuring student and teacher achievement, much less school funding and teacher quality, is a dangerous system indeed."

"Dangerous" is certainly not a synonym for "nourish". I am listening to my gut. It's telling me to get up and leave the theater.

With sincere respect for each of you,
Deborah S. Howard

A month later, Deb told me that she wants to go back to the classroom someday, once all of this reform has been pushed out. I sympathize greatly. Teacher "dropouts" never leave teaching. We all have our individual reasons for doing what we do. I chose to leave so that I could find ways to fight these "reforms" without hearing the threats, but I, same as others like me, hope to return when (and if) things start to move in the direction that our kids need them to.

I love writing and working alongside the activists that are going to turn this around in New York State and across the country. I do enjoy the freedom to be a pain in the ass and be the tiny thorn in the sides of empty suits like Commissioner John King and Stephen Katz, without any fear of retribution. I like being able to support the teachers and parents who come to me for help. I'm not perfect, but I read a lot and I've learned a lot. But I miss teaching.

I miss the feeling of knowing that I'm going to do something great today. I miss the feeling of watching middle school students glow with pride because they figured out how something works, or came up with a new way of doing something. I miss watching kids discover their world and learn how to interact with it effectively. Hell, I even miss bus duty.

I've spoken to countless teachers–actual, working teachers–who miss it just as much as I do. There are so many ridiculous and meaningless mandates and policies that have completely strangled this profession. Teaching is supposed to be a journey, where you get to join several young people as they move through the complexities of the world, stepping in to help them correct the path or encourage them to keep moving. For many, though, it has become worse than just a job. It has become a painful spectatorship of the goals of the wealthy and the powerful.

They miss teaching like I do. I hear it from them every day. Kids miss school, too. I hear them, as well.

I want to teach again someday soon. Many of my currently teaching friends would appreciate being able to teach again soon, too. I want to help get rid of this mess and the people who made it. I want to see a teacher uprising to meet the parent uprising that is still growing. Maybe it's starting to happen.

As Christine McCarthy, a New Yorker who currently teaches in Finland, says:

> These teachers who leave by resignation or retirement are not to be chastised for their decisions. They had their reasons. And now, many of us are using our time and our freedom to rally against the enemies of our profession. We can't help wondering, however, how to get the voices of those still in the trenches to get louder and come together.

Badass

In addition to the local teacher groups and the actions we're seeing from local union chapters, I think we are also starting to see a more aggressive teacher response across the nation. In late June, Professor Mark Naison, who teaches African-American History courses at Fordham University in New York City, joined forces with teachers Priscilla Sanstead and Marla Kilfoye to launch a presence on the Internet called the Badass Teachers Association.

Using the initial from the first two words, they came to call their members BATs, using the feared animal as a symbol that teachers aren't to be messed with, and that the corporate and government reformers have reason to fear. The group grew at an unprecedented rate during its first few weeks on social media, and within a month had over 23,000 members. Why did it grow so fast?

Their mission statement gives a pretty good indication:

> *Badass Teachers Association was created to give voice to every teacher who refuses to be blamed for the failure of our society to erase poverty and inequality through education. BAT members refuse to accept assessments, tests and evaluations created and imposed by corporate driven entities that have contempt for authentic teaching and learning.*

Of course, like any new and rapidly growing nationwide movement, there have been growing pains. As things start to settle down, though, I expect to see a push for fairness, local control, and a respect for the true professionals of the field. And, as the state branch-offs start to grow in tandem, we will see even more.

Obviously, there has been some concern over the group's title, as some (but by no means most) teachers feel uneasy about associating with such a risqué and seemingly unprofessional name. But most members support the name and wear it with pride. Teachers are known for their image of purity and polite consent to whichever way the political winds blow. These days, however, these honorable traits may have been partly to blame for the ability of strong-arm politicians and corporations to take over our profession and try to drive us out. It's time to take a different approach. As founder, Dr. Naison, states, teachers are tired of being scapegoats for all of society's ills.

> *We've had enough. We are not your doormats. We are not your punching bags. We are some of the hardest working, most idealistic people in this country and we are not going to take it anymore. We are going to stand up for ourselves and stand up for our students, even if no organization really supports us. We are Badass. We are legion. And we will force the nation to hear our voice!*

It resonates from the voices of the Seattle and Hamburg teachers, who did what they knew they had to do for the good of their students and their colleagues, even if no one else stood beside them. That's why these reforms that are taking over our nation's schools will not work. These terrible ideas to take over the nation's teachers, schools, and the minds of kids will ultimately fail, because there are two very powerful and very determined groups that will fight to protect our kids: *parents and teachers.*

Push them hard enough, and they will push back harder.

And those two groups—parents and teachers—have another partner in their corner, which is beginning to organize and grow in numbers. All across the country we're seeing public school students find their voices, find their allies, and protest the injustices they see in their schools and neighborhoods every day.

The Locals, Dropouts, and BATs

CHAPTER

6

Our Kids

Across the country, yet somehow hidden from mainstream media, student boycotts, protests, and walkouts have also occurred to show how our kids feel about being pigeonholed into narrow curricula, having their budgets cut and teachers fired, and tested to the extreme. Stories from Denver, Seattle, New York, California, Chicago, Florida, New Jersey, and Portland, Oregon, have been passionate, eye-opening, and heart-wrenching. The saddest part, however, is that no one seems to know about them.

Here are a few of the student actions that made headlines this past school year. I hope to see many more in the year and years to come.[82]

Oregon Students Protest and Walk Out

In February 2013, following the Seattle teacher boycott, Portland-area students decided it was time for them to make their voice heard as well. Dozens of students picketed the Portland

Public Schools district office to protest proposed budget cuts and the expensive and flawed Oregon Assessment of Knowledge and Skills (OAKS) test. Portland district personnel responded by saying that they cannot force a child to take a test, but that they are bound by law to administer that test, and they will continue to do so. Similar to other states, students do have the option to refuse to take a state-mandated standardized test, but that's not all the students were fighting.

The most destructive part of the test for students, other than the fact that it unfairly puts their teachers' jobs and their school buildings at risk, is the fact that districts and schools spend way too much money and time on preparation for those tests. Test prep booklets (usually published by the test developers themselves) are pricey, and precious instructional time is wasted both during prep and testing periods. The Seattle communities knew that, and more and more students, teachers, and parents are waking up to that reality.

Students in Oregon also wanted to know why their state and districts are cutting budgets for essential and elective programs and still increasing the budgets for testing materials and time. Unfortunately, every time that question is asked, there is never any real answer. State and district offices love to give canned answers to try to relate how important the testing is to students' futures, while the rest of us shake our heads at their complete ignorance or denial of the truth. Portland high school students know that their futures depend on the enrichment they seek in authentic learning environments and programs, not on low-level, one-size-fits-all state tests.

As a short aside, I have seen the computer-administered OAKS test, which is almost always administered in computer labs and are not, by any means, secure. It's silly that teachers in Atlanta, Washington, D.C., and elsewhere are being investigated for cheating, while states, like Oregon, are not investigated for their use of unsecure tests and testing environments.

Zombies in Providence and Charlotte

On April 9, 2013, zombies invaded downtown Charlotte, North Carolina, to protest the upcoming state standardized tests. The "zombies" were Charlotte Mecklenburg Schools students who wanted to make a statement about what they see in their classrooms. Assisted by the Mecklenburg ACTS group, students dressed up in tattered clothing, creepy make-up, and mussed hair to show how preparing for these tests makes them feel, and to describe the tests themselves.

"They're mindless and they just keep coming," much like zombies in Hollywood, says Pam Grundy, who co-chairs the ACTS. "They just keep coming, though it's been proven that these tests don't lead to academic improvement." Pam told me in a meeting in the Fall of 2012 that everyone with a background in standardized testing knows that they are efficient at testing one thing, and one thing only: affluence or lack thereof.

As of this writing, North Carolina parents, students, and teachers have engaged in no less than a half-dozen Moral Monday protests at the state capital in Raleigh, in which the zombies have begun to march again. The new state budget bill that passed recently denies teacher career status, freezes teacher salaries (for the sixth or seventh year in a row), denies higher pay for extra credentials, and increased the Teach for America budget by about $6 million. In other words, North Carolina's government has decided to make it easy to replace teachers based on student test scores, which also means that there will be *more* standardized testing, fewer classroom materials, and less instructional time during the day.[83] The zombies will rise again to show the state leadership what they think of this system. Soon, they will be speaking Rhode Island's message below.

Prior to the Charlotte demonstration, students in Providence, Rhode Island staged their own zombie protest, but with a slightly different message. Rhode Island requires high school seniors to take and pass a summative exam before they are to receive a diploma. The protesters want the public and their elected representative that the test is a cumulative exam that does not show a comprehensive picture of the progress, achievement, or abilities of graduates.

Rhode Island students want the state department to know that these tests threaten their futures, for without a diploma, "They take away our life, make us undead," in the words of a Providence high school student.

Denver Students Walk Out

In Denver, Colorado, students staged several walkouts to protest the Transitional Colorado Assessment Program (TCAP) tests, which they believe are harmful to the students, the teachers, and the curriculum in Denver. Alex Kacsh is one of the organizers of Students4OurSchools, a fledgling association of students who want to make themselves part of the conversation of how education works in Colorado.

Although the protest groups have been small, the message has been loud and clear, and Kacsh hopes to see the movement grow. These students aren't just protesting tests, either, they are also providing alternative ideas for student assessment. Kacsh believes that portfolio-based and authentic assessments are the best ways for students to show what they know and what they can do. Standardized testing is very narrow and of little utility.

I've met with Kacsh twice—once at the Occupy D.O.E. rally in D.C. and once at my presentation in Douglas County, Colorado— and I know he is still highly dedicated to creating change for the students who come after him. Along with Nikhil Goyal's recent call for a nationwide student boycott of standardized tests for the 2013-2014 school year, Kacsh is finding ways to rally the troops even more.

We would do well to start heeding the words of our youth, instead of marginalizing them as we tend to do. Let them speak and let them act. Let them be part of the change that they (and we) wish to see. As many New York parents have said over the past year, taking part in civil disobedience is a greater learning experience than anything those tests can provide.

Chicago Students Fight for Their Lives

In April of 2013, hundreds of Chicago students walked out of the standardized state testing for many of the same reasons that students around the country did. Chicago students are having a very rough time, thanks to the policies and unethical decisions made by the Chicago Public Schools and Mayor Rahm Emanuel. These sum of these policies can only be called what they really are: racist and classist. They target the poor and the non-white students throughout Chicago, having closed over 50 schools this year in predominantly black and low-income neighborhoods and, most recently, firing over 2,000 school staff members in the same areas. Not only is the heartless Emanuel part of the Chicago Club and one of Obama's favorite reformers, but CPS CEO Barbara Byrd-Bennett is a full-blown Broadie (a graduate of a Broad superintendent academy)—and at the same time she runs the Chicago schools into the ground, she is also on the Broad Foundation's payroll as an Executive Coach, which means that she trains other CEOs and superintendents to be as cold and heartless as she is.

Like many school districts, including the ones I've written about in this chapter, kids are the ones who feel the tangible effects and damage of education reform, especially when those in power start closing their schools and firing their best teachers. In Chicago, a city already suffering through its share of violence and other poverty-related illnesses, kids are learning the hard way that this is only going to get worse. But, they are also the only demographic that really saw this coming and knew that theirs would be the lives most affected.

In closing neighborhood schools, Rahm Emanuel made it necessary to bus or otherwise transport displaced kids to other schools. In a large city with a stubborn gang problem, that can be dangerous. Kids that are associated, correctly or not, with one territory are being forced to travel through rival turf to get to school. This is a recipe for disaster, which has already resulted in violence and shootings.

When the Chicago Teachers Union (CTU) took to the streets in protest, parents and students joined them. Young children have taken to the mic to express how they feel and what they want to happen. Their stories and their pleas are tearjerkers for those of us who understand their situation and who care. Even though the local media has done a good job of showcasing these speeches, they have mostly fallen on deaf ears.

Also, teenagers have been consistently showing up to Chicago Public Schools board meetings, where they want to make their points and ask their questions to Barbara Byrd-Bennett and the board (which seems to do only what she commands). Often, the students create flash mobs of one-liners, chants, and even a few songs, which gets them forcefully removed by security or police personnel. As far as I know, there have been no arrests. Why do kids feel so strongly?

Because they realize that their lives depend on stopping the horrendous policies that are closing their schools and putting their neighborhoods and their safety at risk.

One of the most memorable speeches during the recent July protests came from nine-year-old Asean Johnson, who wanted the school board to know that, "You are slashing our education. You're pulling me down. You're taking our educational opportunities away." As tears streamed down his face, he pleaded with the CPS board to try to realize who needs these schools the most. "I'm a student myself and I'm pleading and begging that you help these parents who are low-income. Give them what they need. Give them these schools."[84] I can't help wonder if the board members looked Asean in the eye during this testimony. If so, did they show warmth or compassion? Or did they stare at him with the same cold, dead eyes I picture in my head?

In *Children of the Core*, I described a school in Salem, Oregon, where the students took pride in developing and maintaining mostly volunteer-led community services for those who would otherwise not be able to afford them. In Chicago, the situation is much the same, but the leaders are actively taking away those services by closing the buildings. While Emanuel and Byrd-Bennett spin the closings as a necessary service to the community, the realities are causing those living in Chicago to face real strife and real harm. And real fear. Schools in urban, low-income neighborhoods are often the lifelines of those neighborhoods, and defunding and closing those schools shoves the area into an unstable and deteriorating spiral very quickly.

Chicago will remain active, and the students are positioning themselves to be the forefront of protests. Watch Chicago closely. If students (and parents and teachers) copied the actions of Chicago protestors across the country, it would be very difficult to ignore.

Tonawanda Valedictorian: The One Number That Matters

As she stood in front of hundreds of peers, parents, teachers, and school officials, Tonawanda's valedictorian delivered a very different type of speech. Rather than give a drawn-out motivational spiel or talk about the future in which she and her peers would be expected to fit, she spoke against the things that she saw happening in her high school due to overtesting.[85]

The speech, which I invite you to watch in its entirety (with closed captioning on), made it very clear that high school students realize that test prep, test taking, and test scores with have no appreciable effect on their future lives. This young woman suggests that those numbers (test scores) do not matter, and that there is only one number that really matters to her at that moment: the phone number of her state representative's office. The phone number was also the title of her speech, so it would be easy for those attending the graduation ceremony to find later.

At about the same time, the graduating class of Columbia University's Teachers College protested the keynote speech given by the New York Board of Regents Chancellor, Merryl Tisch, at their ceremony. Graduates silent held up signs, which read "Not a

Test Score" during her presentation. I hope that made her nervous or, at least, flustered and annoyed.

The kids and future teachers who get it and who can see what's happening are brave to stand up for their peers and their future students by speaking publicly against the system. It makes me happy and proud to see more and more of them break away from the sit-down-and-shut-up confines of standardized learning and speaking truth to power. If you are or know of a student who is frustrated by the way things are going, I encourage action. Students, just like the rest of us, can find power in numbers and have the right to raise their voices for change.

Natalie Educates the Community

In July, a PowerPoint presentation started making the Internet rounds, which has been used several times to educate members of the community and beyond about the realities, fears, and implications of the Common Core in secondary public schools. When I saw the slides, I recognized many of the facts that are shared among those in the know, and of which many in the general public are still not aware. It was obvious that the creator of the presentation had done his or her homework and had some pretty impressive design skills, too.

What took me by surprise was that the slides and the accompanying lecture were researched, created, and published by a 13-year-old girl from Missouri. After watching carefully and asking the right questions to the right people, Natalie decided that her school was not being run the way that she knew best served her interests. I had a chance to ask Natalie some questions, and her answers reflect her intelligence and her drive. I wanted to know what had pushed her to become active, what her peers and others thought of her activism, and what types of changes she has seen in her school over the past few years. Here are her words about why she's stepping up and speaking out:

I am active because I am a truth teller. I don't like the federal government trying to tell me how I should learn. What drove me to make the presentation is the fact that I am an experiment in education. This is an experiment. This is also against my 10th amendment right. The fact that the government thinks they can go against my rights is not okay. I like to be my own person. Not 'common'. I don't want to be like anyone else. I don't want to learn like every state and every school district.

Since Natalie is in middle school, I had to know what others were saying about her activism, especially her friends and teachers. Social pressure to fit into certain molds and cliques is pretty heavy at this age, and Natalie has plenty of friends. I was curious how they respond to her tendency to speak out against things she didn't think were fair.

My friends always ask me, "Why do you care?" Because they've been taught to sit down, be comfortable, and don't worry about anything. It will be okay. That's wrong though. It's up to my generation to fix things. It's important that people stand up for what they believe in. Let's walk the walk.

When it comes to teachers, it depends on the teacher. I've had teachers tell me, "You're one-minded, and one-sided. You need to be more educated." My teachers complain that I am "too opinionated." Some of my teachers don't respect that I'm allowed to have an opinion, and I am allowed to speak my mind. One time, my math teacher would not let me tell my side of Common Core. I tried and tried and she told me, "You're not educated enough." That night I went home and did seven hours' worth of research. So I tried and tried to tell her, and she still did not answer. So I ended up interrupting her, and told her my opinion and the facts on it. Her last words to me were, "Thank you for that Natalie." I didn't know if I should be offended that she didn't respond or if I should take it as a compliment that she had no response.

My principals respect my opinions and encourage me to be my own person. I am my own person and I won't let anyone—not my teachers, not my friends, not anyone—tell me who to be and what to say. My parents raised me and taught me from a young age to be unique and to be an original. Not a copy. One of my favorite quotes is "Be yourself because everybody else is already taken."

Finally, Natalie told me about the changes that she has seen in her school and the way things are taught.

A lot has changed in my school. One thing that I really notice is that everything has to be explained. Meaning, we have to explain how we got 5 x 5. We have to explain how we got 45/5. It's micromanaged and all about the data at school.

One year we had so many tests to take, that my teacher was so flustered. She ended up having me put every grade in the grade book and do all her scoring. It's always test after test, and example after example. My teacher would complain to me that she couldn't do anything fun to teach us. She always said, "I have too many tests to hand out in such a short amount of time. I can't teach you guys anything in a fun way. I have to teach it to you quick." Schools are losing control quickly. They're losing good teachers, because there's too much pressure. It's time we learn what the problem is and fix it, instead of making it even bigger, with things like Common Core.

As a math teacher, I always thought it was important that my students had a conceptual understanding of why certain things worked the way they work. I very often hear students and parents complain about long it takes to do math homework with curriculum aligned to the Common Core, simply because there is so much explaining and writing and drawing and more explaining. While I still believe that conceptual understanding is important, Natalie would agree with me that it has become the focus and that it's way overdone. It's become a headache and a frustration for students, teachers, and parents alike.

The thing is, students don't need to prove their conceptual understanding with every single problem, every single time. That's overkill, and it takes up valuable time, which students should be using to develop fluency as well. Having taught and trained with the materials that Pearson creates for the Common Core Math Standards, I can attest that there is entirely too much explaining, and much of the explaining is difficult because students generally just want to attribute answers to things like common sense or general knowledge or "because I can see!"

I know that teachers agree with Natalie also, because they know they are short on time as they teach a very time-consuming curriculum, which is aligned to very numerous standards. Teachers also know when their kids get it, and it's pretty insulting to take that power out of a teacher's hands and put it into a scripted curriculum that has "acceptable" and "unacceptable" answer templates. We don't need those. We know what we're doing.

Natalie did her research and found out things that made her uneasy about how the system was treating her. Smart kids don't want to be experimental guinea pigs and they certainly don't want to feel pigeonholed into selected categories of equal outcomes. Natalie knows her potential and her worth as an individual and she will fight for her right to keep that worth. We should expect no less from any of the children in our schools and in our lives.

Back to Basics and Forward to Exceptionalism

CHAPTER

7

Back to Basics and Forward to Exceptionalism

So, what is the fix? What are all of these people—the moms and dads, the civic groups, the teachers, the students—fighting for? In a very compact nutshell, we're fighting for our future. We're fighting to return what is rightfully ours to its rightful place. Public education belongs to us, not them. That's why it's called *public* education. All of those names and organizations you read about in chapter two have one or more agendas at play, which have very little to do with children. Whether for money or power or both, they are willing to experiment, coerce, cajole, and buy their ways into the system that promises a return on their investments. It's an attempt to change *public* education into *corporate* education.

The worst part is, if it all fails and ruins the lives of millions of children, the elite is no worse off for it. If there's one thing they've learned from the past several years, it's that the American government will always side with the rich and powerful. We won't let scandalous banks or dying corporations fail, but we apparently hold no qualms about allowing our kids to fail. We want our large corporations to become the most revered (and feared) in the world, and we apparently will allow them to purchase our children on that market to be used as their labor force. In other words, we've come to expect American billionaires and corporations to be exceptional, not American citizens.

Somewhere along the line, we decided it was okay for the power elite in the United States to self-preserve, while allowing the hard challenges and solutions to go by the wayside. The average citizen-taxpayer in this country has no choice but to go to work every single day, earn a subpar salary, and pay the bills. Missing a day of work can be disastrous for many, since benefits like sick days and healthcare have increasingly become a luxury. Most Americans live in debt, and more and more find themselves living close to or under the poverty line. More and more Americans find themselves forced to accept wages close to the minimum wage in order to pay off debts—some were the citizens' fault, some were the products of corporate games, and some were procured prior to losing a job or taking a cut in salary.

It's no wonder that we can't seem to find the time to educate ourselves about the things happening around us that will end up making it all worse. It's no wonder that so many of us can only use the small amount of free time in our lives to get our news from corporate-sponsored media that feeds us what it wants to know.

It's no wonder that American citizens can't find the time or energy to practice our right to assemble, protest, or strike. If we do, we fall behind. It's no accident. Yes, we did let this happen to ourselves to an extent. When we weren't paying attention to the snakes in the grass or the stealth movements of the wolves behind the trees, they were busy setting up the future they want to see. And we're not part of the club that gets to decide what that future looks like.

Before NCLB (and even during those years, for some), public education was moving along quite well in many places under locally controlled entities, such as districts. With local determination of how children learn, taking into account what regional backgrounds they had and what resources were afforded them, schools and teachers worked together to figure out the best course of action. Local and state universities advised regional districts. Specialists from regional businesses and industries held information sessions in the classrooms and career days. We took field trips—Midwest students may have visited very different places than New York City students—and that made sense. Teachers had the autonomy and trust to understand, guide, and teach their students.

It wasn't perfect, as so many will be dying to say. I know that. If it were, we wouldn't have seen movies like *Dangerous Minds*, *Lean on Me*, and *Stand and Deliver*, where a sole superhero turns around a group of disadvantaged kids living amid violence, poverty, and drugs, and leads them to enlightenment. But that doesn't mean we weren't trying. Some will argue that there has already been too much time and money wasted on things that simply didn't work, and now it's time for something radical and big. We've heard that before too.

Troubled schools in poor and often violent neighborhoods have seen programs and tools and resources and people and every other sort of intervention come around the corner with a short-lived and ineffective plan, but they were never given a true opportunity to try any of them to the best of their abilities. Veteran teachers have often told me that there was always a new mayor or a new education program or something else that put the brakes on programs—some of them actually started showing promise—in order to fulfill a new agenda. Our poorest students have been guinea pigs for a very long time. The only people to take the blame in those schools are the teachers, who have been stretched, abused, and scapegoated the whole time. The bureaucrats, politicians, and corporate investors are long gone and never look back, while the teachers stick around to try to manage the damage caused by temporary and ill-advised initiatives.

It's different this time. This time, the teachers are not just being used to try new experiments and blamed for the failures; teachers are being actively removed from the system or reprogrammed to fit. Those who do speak up or get too rebellious find themselves unemployed before too long. The kids that they worked so hard to support and educate find themselves under the supervision of inadequately prepared recruits that don't have the backgrounds or the knowledge to really meet the challenges and make the difference.

This is what has to stop. And it won't be easy, but it might be quick if enough pressure and resistance is built. From many angles, it appears that Race to the Top and the corporate system surrounding our schools relies on public support (or apathy), and that's where the marketing and propaganda has been focused. What we need to do is continue to grow the resistance. There are two fundamental groups, as I've mentioned too many times before, that need to fight back en masse: parents and teachers. When enough of us stand firm and refuse to allow this corporate takeover to continue, we will see the day when it finally topples.

It's been difficult to motivate people to take action. The one common thing that leads people to get angry is the idea that this is negatively affecting our children—those little people who rely on us to protect them and guide them. When people stop and think about the current attacks on public education and what those things are doing to our children, it makes them angry or scared or both. The actions stop, it appears, when people start thinking that this is all too big and there's nothing that they can do about it. I also think that it's too easy to dismiss this as just another education program of the year, and it will go away soon enough— only to be replaced by the next one in line. I hope I've made the case that that's not going to happen.

By showcasing some of the things that brave parents, teachers, and students have been doing around the country to fight for the future, I hope to give others some models to follow in their own communities. The previous chapters showed some actions in which people can engage to start creating resistance in their own neighborhoods, so that we can start getting back to building an education system that works. I'll get to that in a few pages.

Real Stakeholders are the Bedrock of Change

In July, I spoke to a fairly large group of parents and teachers in Douglas County, Colorado, which is a relatively affluent community south of Denver. This is a district where nothing was broken. In fact, it has been what many called a "model district," where kids had prospects to good colleges, good jobs, and a chance to be the movers and shakers of the future. This district never became victim to the plagues of public education and it was never considered a cautionary tale of some so-called status quo.

But now, that district is in trouble. Douglas County School District is now in the hands of a superintendent and a board of education that has ultimately decided to turn a highly-performing education system into a grand experiment in privatization in suburban schools. Considering the goals of the Broad, Walton, Gates, and other foundations, it's not surprising and it had to happen sometime, somewhere. It just so happened that an election inserted a privatization-motivated board, which was heavily supported by corporate funding.

Let me clarify something. The fact that these board members identify with the Republican Party has nothing to do with the agenda. This could just as easily have been a Democrat-aligned board. The reasons for the partisanship were that the demographics of the community tend to lean towards voting

Republican and that the board members themselves were funded by organizations or individuals that are either supported by the American Legislative Exchange Council (ALEC) or strongly influenced by that group. This is apparent in the strong anti-union and pro-voucher rhetoric coming from those members. Strangely, most parents and teachers in the community support public schools and unionized teachers, and most people close to the district's internal workings have suggested that there is no problem with the union.

Regardless, the board has voted to cut all ties with the union and has effectively outlawed collective bargaining. Again, not because the union was being belligerent or hard to get along with; it was simply a move to keep any resistance at bay while setting up the strong corporate practices inside the district policies.

Superintendent Elizabeth Fagen has praised the new corporate-style merit-based pay system, which she claims is the answer to the "broken step-and-lane" system of teacher pay. She claims that the old system rewards bad teachers, while her new system (which completely discounts certification levels, prior experience, or education attainment) will allow teachers to be hired at the entry level and work their up the ladder to become leaders themselves.

This system has never been shown to have any effectiveness in any school, anywhere. The worst part is that districts like Douglas County had an opportunity to make real and historic changes that would put them on the map as the country's most innovative district, with the most advanced methods of schooling and development. Using their unbroken and strong foundation, they easily could have tweaked some things here, tried some news things there, and grown into a true stakeholder-led powerhouse of learning. Instead, they chose to let corporate money and hardline Republicans crack that foundation and run (or ruin) their future.

This brings me to the point of this final chapter: there are many groups of people who believe that we should be using corporate practices to make schools more fiscally efficient; I believe it's time we stop seeking the ruinous corporate practices and return to *best practices*. We can be both efficient and effective; we were doing a really good job, as I mentioned earlier, until the corporate takeover created an environment that was neither efficient nor effective. More importantly, though, we can return to making public education's primary goal all about the most important thing in parents' and teachers' lives: the happiness and development of our children.

Shareholders want to create profits; stakeholders want to see success. Stakeholders want to see the system work well and they want to know they are a vital part of it and that it will work well for them and their kids. To suggest that the Gates, Walton, Broad, and Friedman Foundations are stakeholders is completely incorrect. Stakeholders seek a system that will stabilize and open up every opportunity for every child. That isn't easy and there's no silver bullet, regardless of what the current reform movement says.

Parents want their kids to be happy. Kids want to be engaged and moved towards happiness and the realizations of their dreams. Teachers want to go home at night and the end of the school year knowing that their work is meaningful and essential. Universities want well-prepared, thoughtful, creative, and able students to join their research ranks. And communities want to know that they will see a new generation of entrepreneurs, change agents, leaders, and intelligent citizens moving into the spaces the last generation left open.

Something very big has to happen first, and if we do this intelligently and we put the power and the policy back into the right hands, it may sting for a while but it won't be that hard to accomplish. Ready?

Moving Towards a Better Way

Before I start getting into the way things need to change for the better, let me make a suggestion that won't be popular with some of the more libertarian or small-government supporters. We cannot simply eradicate the Federal Department of Education. Before closing the book and walking away, however, hear me out. I *do believe strongly* that we should pressure our leaders to strip it down to only a few essential services. As an example, it's still necessary to maintain the Education Department's Office for Civil Rights for pretty depressing yet realistic reasons. If the recent charter school takeovers have been any indication, maintaining equality in education is still a problem that needs to be monitored and evaluated. Even when the charter companies promise to serve children with troubled backgrounds, behavioral records, or special needs, we've seen too many times that they certainly don't really mean it.

If I may also be frank, there are certain parts of this country where the leaders who make educational policy decisions do not recognize the importance or necessity of equality. In general, the stakeholders (teachers, parents, and students) will always advocate for all children, regardless of circumstance or gender or race or disability, but there must remain entities that will step in and reinforce that advocacy. Until our fringe political minorities— and the legislators that cater to them—all grow up a little more, this is the reality.

There are also departments at the Federal level which are still necessary but in need of serious overhaul. I would suggest that this statement represents the majority of those offices. Federal Student Aid, state funding, Title I, limited-English proficiency (LEP), IDEA, and ethnicity-based programs need to be closely scrutinized and either fixed or reorganized. I agree with most of my conservative friends and many of my liberal friends who suggest that the Education Department has become entirely too bloated, self-preserving, and headed in the completely wrong direction.

It's simplistic, unrealistic, and radically wrong to suggest that the Federal Department of Education should be scrapped entirely, though.

What also needs to happen very quickly and completely is the end of Federal control over teaching and learning methodologies and practices. Contests for "innovation" may have sounded like a cute idea to Arne Duncan, but we all knew what the real design was about. If the Federal government wants to start throwing contests around, it should be in a fiscal environment where schools aren't suffering from budget crises, and where the choice to participate in those games is truly a *choice*. To watch the educational infrastructure crumble under a weak economy and targeted attacks, and then tell states that a "voluntary" contest will get them some extra cash is not just disingenuous, it's flat out unethical and harmful. And it's ultimately hurting our children more than anyone else.

We also need to keep the corporate money from influencing legislation and policy that puts public schools under the thumb of Federal and corporate power. It's time to fight ALEC, Citizens United, and any other entity that promotes this unethical behavior.

So, one way we're going to start making public education more efficient (which is the word that corporations love to use to describe low overhead and high productivity outcomes) is to get rid of the Federal control and corporate influence of teaching and learning.

What else increases our efficacy and efficiency?

I've been saying for a very long time that child-led and teacher-guided methodologies (e.g. Montessori) must be integrated into traditional schools, with the intent of making public schools less common and less standard. If anything, we should be giving states and districts the freedom and ability to try truly innovative practices, which they can research and evaluate independently, and then publish their successes and opportunities for improvement. Bill Gates keeps calling the current "reform" movement "science-based." I think we should try some real science, by letting community education stakeholders design, create, and test their own best practices and methods and submit them into an idea marketplace, where those stakeholders can see what's working and what's not. And there should be no financial or legislative strings attached.

Outcome-based education, data-driven learning, and other such fancy terms have led us down a bad road. Kids are not simple little machines that can be measured using quick, cheap, and singular data points. We need to do better, we need to stop trying to make it national and common, and we need to stop tying high stakes to the outcomes. Teacher performance is not in a directly correlative relationship with student test scores. That's the reality.

Most importantly, though, we need to go back to a system where teams of teachers and specialists are able and expected to develop methods of evaluation for themselves and their students. As I've discussed, when teachers are allowed to reflect on and perfect their craft, they will. And they'll do it without much pressure from the outside or the top tier of leadership. Teachers are learners and performers; they want to know how to get better, and they'll work hard to get better. We are no longer cogs in the "factory model" education machine. We've been educated and trained to use our resources and the prevailing research in ways that were never considered in the past. We are the best source of education that our kids have. We are the best choice for the majority of American children and families.

Do I support choice in the American school system? Of course I do! I do not, however, accept as valid what so many politicians and lobbyists and education venture capitalists call "choice." Remember, in the late 1990s and early 2000s, we had charter schools popping up within public school systems that were sometimes led by leadership that had a genuine concern for meeting the needs of the communities in which they operated. Several of those schools fell apart within the first few years for various reasons, but I think they were onto something good and real. Unfortunately, corporatization schemes got involved and the models became saturated with business lingo and practice.

The charter schools we see today are not "choices" or "alternatives." They are designed to be replacements for whole-child education centers and they are designed to be workforce training centers for the list of cronies in chapter 2. The "voucher" and "parent trigger" laws being pushed by so many state leaders are not created for the best interests of kids, they are pushed for the greater interest of their corporate and rich investors.

I do believe that student and family choice should be built into the public school system, at the community level, by master teachers and administrators who work closely with local and regional universities and businesses. Schools are not just centers for workforce training; schools are centers for community building. That doesn't mean that students are only responsible for preparing themselves for life within that community, and it doesn't mean that the word community has to represent a limited area. That's why we need to invent and maintain a system of public education that fosters and promotes authentic choice— freely and equitably.

In a nutshell, we can have both strong public school systems *and* the reality of school choice, all in one cohesive package. And without the intrusion of the entities that wish to control it all and profit from it.

If we are serious about the investments in our kids' brighter and more successful futures, the ability to broaden their horizons and their choices, based on their own dreams and abilities, this will be a reality. Even in smaller communities, the talent and the drive to differentiate authentic instruction exists in almost every teacher, and can be harnessed strategically to give students and families *real* choices in education. Why hasn't this been a part of the discussion lately? Of course, the obvious answer here is that corporate education reform and the race to remain economically dominant doesn't seem to recognize children as the key to a growing community of learners and creators. Instead, as this book hopefully spelled out, there is a small but powerful army of control freaks who wish to create the next generation of low-wage and low-power workers. And, quite frankly, it's very difficult to corporatize or profit from such a democratic system.

But, what about the rest of us? Why aren't we *all* seeing through the hyperbole and the snake oil?

I think it's because we don't have the answers and therefore feel powerless to suggest what's next. This is a false crisis, as well.

We have plenty of people who have the vision and the skills to build what should happen next. The vision of the future shouldn't be technology-led learning or corporate-created drones; the future of education shouldn't be nationally mandated or based on content standards; the future *should* be child-led, with an ever broadening network of paths for students to follow as they begin to age and realize their potentials and self-chosen destinations.

Imagine a system where all students were led to use and understand basic skills, in order to build their literacy in reading, mathematics, and science—at the pace of their abilities—alongside general understanding. There's no reason to ask a second grader to construct understanding of concepts for which there is no background or for which that child's cognitive development is not ready. There's no reason to push skills onto children who don't have the cognitive readiness or the ability to see how those skills are relevant or meaningful. We can't do that to them, and we certainly can't do that to *all* of them at *all* the same time.

What we can do is create an environment where young students are able to use their own faculties and their own backgrounds (with guidance from real-world experiences and qualified mentors) to learn the fundamental knowledge that we deem necessary to live in this world and its many different communities. That means basic arithmetic, the ability to not only read but love reading, the ability to write well, and the ability to approach new problems and situations without fear and with enthusiastic confidence. Regardless of what the "hard life" people keeping saying, students (especially young ones) should not be suffering symptoms of anxiety about going to school.

Organic and educator-led reform is what will work for our kids and our country. Corporate reform is the anti-science that will serve only the investors and the elite.

My friend, Nora McNamara, a child and adolescent psychiatrist, wraps up neatly what our aim should be:

> *What all of us hope for our children is to learn how to learn, and to love learning. What all of us who study human neurocognitive development know is that human children learn best in an environment with multi-aged peers, with a teacher ("Guide") who can get to know them over multiple years, and where the Guide is able to observe individual children and present lessons tailored to that child's need, and with the opportunity to explore outside the classroom environment to support that child's passion(s).*

It sounds so radical! That's the reaction you'll hear often from traditional-minded education leaders and practitioners who had been working towards this type of system without even really knowing it, probably. Well, they were working towards it before the current bulldozing of our profession. We educate hearts and minds, not robotic data systems that must learn how to do what the top-down prescriptions tell them. Our kids should be ready to think and feel their way through the things that life throws at them. They should be able to use the soft skills and academic learning they've acquired and practiced to face the world ahead.

They should have a background that is broad as well as solid, and which they've helped build, in order to become a part of the community in which they choose to live.

They should be allowed and expected to fail over and over and over again, and feel good about it.

There's no accountability! This is the hubris of the unenlightened, the statistics addicts, the policy wonks, and those who really don't have a grasp on how learning and cognition work. Accountability is a term that is synonymous with teacher evaluation. In our current administrative environment, there is actually no accountability for *kids*. If the kids' test scores go up, teachers are rewarded; if the scores go down, teachers are reprimanded, "corrected," or removed. I would suggest that quite the opposite is necessary—there is *more* accountability in the type of system Nora explains above, since individual students will once again become the center of the work we all do for them. And they will be ultimately responsible for the discoveries they make, the work they do, the ideas they conjure, and the things they produce.

This is one of the main problems with the current privatization and charter movement. There is no consistent accountability—at all. In order to sell the plan—closing schools, firing teachers, and taking over school buildings for charters—we have to be sold that the system is being held accountable. If the system is causing a child to fail, then the schools and teachers within must be tossed aside so that a more efficient model can step in and, well, boost test scores (they don't actually do anything else).

Once the takeover has happened, then we see the upside-down flip of all flips. Charter schools are no longer required to show accountability, other than by those test scores, and the children themselves are told and trained over and over that *they*—not teachers or schools or parents—are the ultimate factor in their success. If students can't handle that, they are kicked out of those schools (which are not held accountable at all), to be dealt with by the state and the taxpayers once again.

This is where the really evil part of this plan happens: tell a child and her parents that this new charter system will save her and get her into college. Then, once the lottery chooses her, she is left to her own devices in order to succeed, and is fully accountable for her own progress from that point on. If she fails, it's her fault. The idea of student support in an environment where teachers come and go, and test scores are the golden ticket, is not the same as the idea of support from educated and trained professionals. The accountability is transferred strictly to the child. *Be Nice. Work Hard.* The KIPP model says it all.

Accountability should be a shared responsibility among *all stakeholders*—not just teachers and not just students—and it should not rely on test scores based on shoddy content standards (or *any* content standards, really).

Read a little more about KIPP and their accountability in *Children of the Core*, if you haven't already.

It sounds expensive! One thing I've noticed about school district expenditures is how things are starting to change away from direct instruction (or classroom spending—different places call it different things) and more towards "contracts," "professional services," "instructional resources," or something else like that. Most districts spend between 45% and 60% of their total budgets on direct instruction, which includes teacher salaries. As I moved through a few district budgets in a few states, I noticed that the percentage for direct instruction has been creeping slowly lower, as the contracts percentage (usually around 20%) continues to creep higher.

Costs to districts and states can seemingly only go down once expensive contracts with testing corporations, textbook publishers, and other private services are altered or discontinued. If we don't fire all of the good teachers and administrators too soon, we'll have all of the expertise already employed in our school districts, and I can assure you they'd be happy to start building an education system that works. They will join forces with the ranks of university professors, business leaders, parents, students, and community members who have real stake in education and training and who want to make the future a friendly and forward-moving place for our kids. But there is another fight we have to watch out for.

Facing the Privatization Movement

There is a troubling trend in the growing movement to eradicate the current Obama-led education reforms, about which I've spent most of my time writing. Underneath the surface, there are wolves in sheep's clothing. I've shared the stage and the television screen with a few of those wolves and we've been fighting the same enemy, for now. I can tell, however, that once we've won, a new struggle will rise above the surface for the fate of American public schools.

The misleading movement to promote "parent choice" is one that has been fighting Common Core and national testing alongside those of us who are fighting to save the public schools that serve kids and their neighborhoods. I have read several reports from proponents of school vouchers and parent trigger laws that Common Core is antithetical to what they support and that it forces states to comply with a Federal overreach into states' rights. It's an odd mismatch of strange enemies and stranger bedfellows.

In one corner, we have the extremes I wrote about above—the Tea Party and the Occupy Education movements—working toward the same goal of ending *nationalized* corporate education reform and common standards. I wonder, though, if they were successful in eradicating those things, what would happen next? Tea Parties are generally anti-union and do not support the idea of tax-supported public schools. The Occupy folks tend to be very pro-union and pro-public-funded schools. Would we be able to join in a conversation that allows for free, public, state-level school systems that encourage choice *within* those systems? Would we be supportive of creating an education system that abides by the Constitution and still prepares our kids for success in life?

I can actually visualize such a system, built and supported by all, and I wonder if we are ready to work towards that. Obviously, the existence of private, home, and parochial schools will still be an option, but not at the expense of taxpayers and the families and students that rely on the public schools for more than just education.

Just prior to releasing this book, I spoke at two education conventions in Alabama. I was joined by well-known speakers from The Heartland Institute, The American Principles Project, and the Pioneer Institute. The idea was to educate parents, teachers, and community members on the realities of the Common Core State Standards Initiative and its associated testing culture and data and privacy concerns. We agreed with each other on just about everything we had to say. And my fellow panelists were three of the nicest people I have met. When we parted ways, however, I was reminded that the American Principles Project and the Heartland Institute are both members of the Education Task Force for the American Legislative Exchange Committee (ALEC), which is focused on pushing aside publicly run schools in favor of privately run (but still publicly funded) corporate charter schools—the workforce training centers about which I've written so much—as well as promoting voucher and parent trigger laws, which have no evidence of efficacy and have torn communities apart in the few that have enacted those laws.

I oppose the Common Core because of the reasons I outlined in chapter 3. My new friends oppose Common Core because of many of those same reasons, but also because of its dissonance with their agendas of state-led (as opposed to Federally-mandated) privatization and/or defunding of public schools. In other words, if we ever defeat the common enemy of Common

Core, we will once again be at odds with each other regarding the future of those public schools. The corporate and political players among us don't care one way or another. Sure, the Common Core was designed to create a workforce training system that will flood the job markets with cheap, employable labor meant for large corporations with their eyes on global dominance.

But that doesn't mean the corporate allies of ALEC don't have a "plan B," which is to use the large collection of corporate, trade, and other group members they have amassed in support of their agenda to push the privatization laws through. They intend to win—and to profit—at the expense of our kids, Common Core or no Common Core.

So far, the non-CCSS privatization movement has garnered the support from mostly Republican lawmakers, including Senator Marco Rubio, as well as many state-level legislators. In other words, we're seeing a movement beginning to push for states' rights, which may make it easier for corporate charters to move into states where there either are no standards for accountability, or where those standards are created for the purpose of creating artificial failure, much as we're seeing across the nation now. In some of those states, all they have to do is utter the words "government schools," and many parents are ready to pull the "trigger." Or, at least vote for vouchers.

Perhaps that is better than a nationwide system of common standards, testing, and school takeovers, but the outcome will be the same in the unlucky states. "Choice" will still be a misnomer for the poor, minority kids—especially in urban areas—and that will only result in wider achievement, income, and resource gaps. Those states will see astroturf groups run over their educational systems, leaving the affluent at the top, and the poor at the bottom. Professional, experienced teachers will be devalued and chased away, to be replaced by low-paid and temporary workers. All it takes is a cursory look at the New Orleans, North Carolina, and Chicago messes to see what ideas are brewing there.

Educators, kids, and parents are truly stuck between a corporate rock and a hard place, here.

Instead of becoming adversaries, however, I'm hoping that my conservative and libertarian counterparts and I can begin to see together that instead of replacing public schools with the poorly named "choice system," we must find new and innovative ways to bring real, meaningful *choice* to the public school system. It's the only way to ensure that we are providing a free, quality education to all kids with the common ideals of equality (remember, equality does not have to mean everyone is educated the same; it simply means that everyone is afforded the same opportunities) and open academic opportunities for every single one of our children, from which they can ultimately choose their own destinies. To deny that is to reinvent the very beast we are attempting to slay: a revival of classist and racist policies that leave the poor and minority children behind.

If we use our human and intellectual resources (the real education professionals) that are widespread throughout the country, we can ensure a system built on both equality *and* choice. Vouchers and lotteries are the barriers to such a system, not the answers. Vouchers and lotteries don't exist in upper middle class or affluent areas. This is odd, since the biggest supporters of vouchers and lotteries into private-run charters tend to be upper middle class and affluent voters. It's time we educate those people, who are voting with their parties instead of with good intentions for the kids they know little about.

One last time: we have the people, the talent, and the drive to make public education serve all of our children with the best education in the world. We've been doing that pretty well so far, limited only by the sabotage levied against us by those who wish to bring the system down and buy it out for profit using vouchers, triggers, and school takeovers. Our goal should be to get them out of the way and let the professionals do their work. Our goal should be to ensure that our tax dollars are going to a system that develops and guides our children to success, rather than a system that feeds the corporatocracy in America.

Together, as citizens, we can demand and bring real change and real choice to the children of America. Together, we can allow our students to follow their aptitudes, their dreams, their hopes, and their interests into the future. With that system in place, our next generation will lead us into a future that they help build, rather than corporate interest dragging our kids into a future that they've already planned. I know which future I've chosen for my kids. What about you?

Use the small sampling of activism stories I've collected as your motivation and model. Use the love of your children and your freedom to get active.

Get educated. Get organized. Get busy.

APPENDIX

GET EDUCATED

Learn more about these organizations and programs and their roles in education reform. Start with a Google search.

Achieve, Inc.

ALEC

Amplify

Cory Booker

Eli and Edythe Broad Foundation

Carnegie Foundation

Chicago Public Schools

Common Core State Standards Initiative

Douglas County, CO

Foundation for Excellence in Education (FEE)

Milton Friedman Foundation

Bill and Melinda Gates Foundation

K^{12}, Inc.

Measures of Effective Teaching (MET)

Milton Friedman Foundation

Parent Trigger Laws

Partnership for Assessments of Readiness for College and Careers (PARCC)

Pearson, McGraw-Hill, Common Core, Inc.

Privatization of Schools
Race to the Top
Smarter Balanced Assessment Consortium (SBAC)
StudentFirst
Vouchers and Parent Trigger Laws
Walton Family Foundation

GET ORGANIZED
Badass Parents Association
   https://www.facebook.com/BadassParentsAssociation
Badass Teachers Association (Also Chapters in All 50 States)
   http://www.badassteacher.org/
   http://forum.badassteacher.org/
Parents and Educators Against the Common Core
   http://usagainstcommoncore.blogspot.com/
   https://www.facebook.com/groups/PEACCS/
Parents and Teachers Against the Common Core
   http://p-tacc.blogspot.com/
   https://www.facebook.com/groups/549231011767025/
Students United for Public Schools
   http://studentsunitedforpubliced.org/
New York State Allies for Public Education
   Use this group as a model for action in other states, and use
   the tools to organize house parties, workshops, etc.
    http://www.nysape.org
On Facebook, search for "Stop Common Core" and your state. I
guarantee you'll find a group.

Also, search Facebook for "Opt Out" and your state. I *almost* guarantee you'll find a group.

GET BUSY

The most important thing any one person can do is **educate**. Find ways to organize small or large groups and share the things you've learned from this book, other sources, or from your memberships in groups.

Copy action items that you see from other groups or get creative and make up your own! Action items generally take numbers, so recruit in your own area, but don't be afraid to ask members of other groups for help with your action item. For example, if you want to plan a phone blitz, where you have as many people as possible call the governor of your state, don't be afraid to ask parents and teachers from other states to help out. The Badass Teachers Association is very open to blitzing across state lines and they have a huge membership.

Here are two action items to get you started, which are being planned in many states this year:

The "Send Them Back" Campaign

Not happy with your child's test scores (and the fact that they're bogus, anyway)? SEND THEM BACK!

Change the following to fit your specific state:

Write on the front of the envelope:
"Attention John King: Invalid Test Scores Enclosed"
Commissioner John King
New York State Education Department
89 Washington Avenue
Albany, New York 12234
Let's see how many we can clutter his mailbox with!

If you will not receive scores this year, since you bravely opted out last year, print your schools report card from the district's website and mail that in.

To make it even more effective, send it certified, return-receipt. That way, someone at the district will have to take the time to sign for the delivery.

Opt Out of High-Stakes Tests

The most visible and impactful action parents and students can take is to refuse to participate in high-stakes testing.

High-stakes tests are any tests that are used by the state or district to make decisions about teacher effectiveness, school report cards, or other things that do not pertain to the student and only the student.

High-stakes tests take up way too much instructional time and do no service to the education of your children. By opting out, or boycotting, you are accomplishing quiet civil disobedience to say that testing is useless to teachers, harmful to students, and too expensive. Also, you will be effectively keeping a portion of your child(ren)'s data out of the longitudinal systems.

Find your state guide here: http://www.unitedoptout.com

Then, join an Opt Out of State Tests group on Facebook to get ideas, support, resources, and answers to your questions.

This is going to be a big year!

Notes

NOTES

---

[1] *New York State Testing Program, School Administrator's Manual.* Available at http://www.p12.nysed.gov/assessment/sam/ei-samcc13rev.pdf

[2] http://commonsenseny.blogspot.com/2013/04/ny-state-education-officials-say-take.html

[3] http://www.economist.com/blogs/democracyinamerica/2013/04/standards-based-tests-and-public-schooling

[4] http://www.nytimes.com/2013/04/19/education/common-core-testing-spurs-outrage-and-protest-among-parents.html?_r=1&

[5] http://polhudson.lohudblogs.com/2013/04/11/common-core-is-answer-to-states-problems-education-department-argues-in-video/

[6] http://online.wsj.com/article/SB10001424127887323309604578431263623255902.html

[7] http://cveditorials.com/LI/2013/04/19/common-core-anxiety/

[8] Ibid

[9] Race to the Top Executive Summary. Available at http://www2.ed.gov/programs/racetothetop/executive-summary.pdf

[10] http://www.whitehouse.gov/issues/education/k-12/race-to-the-top

[11] Dear John King: http://atthechalkface.com/2013/04/16/open-letter-to-ny-ed-commissioner-john-king-thank-you/

[12] Stop Privatization of Public Schools website http://dumpduncan.org/

[13] Ibid 10

[14] Ibid 9

[15] http://www.ed.gov/news/press-releases/education-department-announces-

Notes

16-winners-race-top-district-competition

[16] http://www.all4ed.org/resource_lib/links/ncea

[17] http://www.gao.gov/new.items/d1140.pdf

[18] http://www.achieve.org/files/BenchmarkingforSuccess.pdf

[19] http://christienken.com/2013/04/08/translating-the-common-core/

[20] http://voices.washingtonpost.com/answer-sheet/no-child-left-behind/what-is-being-college-and-care.html

[21] http://www.act.org/solutions/college-career-readiness/college-readiness-benchmarks/

[22] http://vonscience.blogspot.com/2006/01/reasons-why-us-should-stay-away-from.html

[23] http://feaweb.org/teach-for-america-study-questioned

[24] http://www.statesmanjournal.com/article/20130804/NEWS/308040048/Closure-teaching-program-Willamette-University-decried

[25] https://www.truth-out.org/news/item/6639-what-100-million-could-do-for-out-of-work-underpaid-teachers

[26] http://www.nextgenscience.org/overview-0

[27] http://seattleeducation2010.wordpress.com/2013/07/02/empire/

[28] http://www.nytimes.com/2009/01/20/us/politics/20text-obama.html?pagewanted=all&_r=0

[29] http://www.washingtonpost.com/blogs/answer-sheet/wp/2013/05/12/gates-gives-150-million-in-grants-for-common-core-standards/

[30] http://www.gatesfoundation.org/media-center/press-

releases/2013/01/measures-of-effective-teaching-project-releases-final-research-report

[31] http://articles.washingtonpost.com/2013-04-24/business/38783974_1_stem-more-foreign-workers-epi-study

[32] http://www.gatesfoundation.org/media-center/speeches/2009/07/bill-gates-national-conference-of-state-legislatures-ncsl

[33] http://www.visasquare.com/visa-greencard/report/exxon-mobil-corporation-69371.html

[34] http://atthechalkface.com/2013/06/11/exxonmobil-sends-mafia-style-letter-to-pa/

[35] http://www.waltonfamilyfoundation.org/educationreform

[36] http://www.dailykos.com/story/2013/04/30/1205905/-Walmart-heirs-invest-8-million-in-StudentsFirst-s-school-privatization-agenda#

[37] Ravitch, Diane. *The Death and Life of the Great American School System: How Testing and Choice Are Undermining Education.* New York: Basic Books, 2010.

[38] http://www.broadeducation.org/about/crisis_stats.html

[39] A Parent Guide to the Broad Foundation's Training Programs and Educational Policies: http://parentsacrossamerica.org/wp-content/uploads/2011/04/PAA-guide-to-the-Broad-Foundation-final-final.pdf

[40] Broad Foundation School Closure Guide: http://failingschools.files.wordpress.com/2011/01/school-closure-guide1.pdf

[41] http://www.susanohanian.org/outrage_fetch.php?id=1589

[42] Model Legislation (lower right on the page): http://www.alec.org/task-forces/education/

[43] http://www.npr.org/2013/06/18/192765776/study-teacher-prep-programs-get-failing-

marks?utm_source=npr&utm_medium=facebook&utm_campaign=20130618

44 http://dianeravitch.net/2013/06/03/what-is-edtpa-and-why-do-critics-dislike-it/

45 http://www.denverpost.com/breakingnews/ci_17350067

46 http://www.governor.ny.gov/press/07082013-governor-announces-applications-for-master-teacher-program
47 http://www.amplify.com/company

48 http://www.nytimes.com/2013/03/06/business/media/news-corp-has-a-tablet-for-schools.html?pagewanted=all&_r=1&

49 http://www.washingtonpost.com/blogs/answer-sheet/wp/2013/03/13/lawsuit-charges-ed-department-with-violating-student-privacy-rights/

50 http://www.educatingflorida.com/marc-tucker.html

51 http://www.ncee.org/

52 http://www.ed.gov/news/speeches/vision-education-reform-united-states-secretary-arne-duncans-remarks-united-nations-ed

53 http://preaprez.wordpress.com/2013/07/19/cps-fired-my-friend-xian-barrett-and-2112-others/

54 From *Wikipedia*: http://en.wikipedia.org/wiki/Jeb_Bush

55 Foundation for Excellence in Education: http://excelined.org/about-us/

56 http://seattleeducation2010.wordpress.com/2012/03/04/a-teacher-says-no-to-common-core-standards/

57 From *Wikipedia*: http://en.wikipedia.org/wiki/David_Coleman_(educator)

58 http://www.pearson.com/michael-barber.html

59 http://pearsonville.com/

[60] http://www.prweb.com/releases/2011/6/prweb8597152.htm

[61] http://en.wikipedia.org/wiki/Joel_Klein

[62] http://atthechalkface.com/2013/07/04/how-aft-and-nea-became-partners-of-corped/

[63] https://inbloom.org/about-inbloom

[64] http://takingnote.learningmatters.tv/?p=6490

[65] http://www.corestandards.org/resources/statements-of-support

[66] http://dianeravitch.net/2013/02/26/why-i-cannot-support-the-common-core-standards/

[67] http://www.uft.org/news-stories/aft-put-high-stakes-use-common-core-tests-one-year

[68] Just like the way that pro-CCSS marketers say that kids will get excited about the new standards and will just love the new way of learning!

[69] http://www.achieve.org/achieving-common-core

[70] http://www.barbarablackburnonline.com/rigor/

[71] http://www.washingtonpost.com/blogs/answer-sheet/wp/2013/01/29/a-tough-critique-of-common-core-on-early-childhood-education/?fb_action_ids=10151508535921161&fb_action_types=og.likes

[72] https://www.google.com/search?q=david+coleman+practice+again+again+again&oq=david+coleman+practice+again+again+again&aqs=chrome.0.69i57j69i62l3.15673j0&sourceid=chrome&ie=UTF-8

[73] http://atthechalkface.com/2013/07/09/oscar-winning-lessons-or-b-movie-scripts-ccss/

[74] Compare SBAC http://sbac.portal.airast.org/practice-test/ to OAKS

http://www.oaks.k12.or.us/students.html

[75] Ibid

[76]
http://money.cnn.com/2013/06/28/technology/innovation/inbloom/index.html

[77] Use of State Test Scores in Teacher and Principal Evaluations
http://shaunpjohnson.files.wordpress.com/2013/08/field-memo-re-scores-release.pdf

[78]
http://www.oms.nysed.gov/press/ELAMathCurricula.SEDAwardsContractsForDevelopment.htm

[79] http://whatiscommoncore.wordpress.com/

[80]
http://colorlines.com/archives/2013/05/victory_for_seattle_teachers_testing_boycott_high_school_map_test_optional_next_year.html

[81] http://www.youtube.com/watch?v=sBSgchJe2Z0

[82] Thanks to Stephanie Rivera for collecting student actions on the Students United for Public Education page: http://studentsunitedforpubliced.org/2013-k-12-student-protests/

[83] http://www.newsobserver.com/2013/07/22/3049030/teachers-say-lawmakers-are-forsaking.html

[84] http://www.huffingtonpost.com/2013/07/24/asean-johnson-school-boar_n_3647474.html

[85] It was requested that I withhold this person's name. Here is the video of the speech that was published on YouTube:
http://www.youtube.com/watch?v=1gcfsTdhS10

About the Author

Kris L. Nielsen has worked in education for over ten years, including six years as a middle grades teacher and instructional leader in New Mexico, Oregon, and North Carolina. He is a graduate of Western Governors University's Master of Science Education program, with emphasis on child development and instructional technology.

Kris is an activist against corporate education reform and continues to write about it and fight along the parents, teachers, and students who want change.

He currently blogs at http://www.atthechalkface.com.

Kris lives in New York State with his wonderful family.